Mary Magdalene Speaks

The Holy Grail, the Bloodline, and

Secrets of the Divine Feminine

By Marcia McMahon, M.A.

To Terry
Marcia McMahon

I

Mary Magdalene Speaks

The Holy Grail, the Bloodline, and

Secrets of the Divine Feminine

ISBN 13: 978-0-97664-774-4

Front cover design: Marcia McMahon

All artwork c. by Marcia McMahon

Editorial services: Mary Mageau, Catherine Cogorno

New explosive truths are revealed at last by Mary Magdalene, Mary the Mother of Jeshua (Jesus Christ), Martha of Bethany, Joseph of Arimathea, and others. In her latest book, *Mary Magdalene Speaks*, author and channel Marcia McMahon, exposes many of the myths surrounding the life of Jeshua, his marriage to Mary Magdalene, their Bloodline, the Divine Feminine, and the Holy Grail.

This book is a must read for all seekers of spiritual truth and I highly recommend it.

Mary Mageau, author and editor

* * * * *

Review for *Mary Magdalene Speaks*, by Joanna Prentis D. hyp

Author, *Power of the Magdalene*, co-author with Stuart Wilson

This book written by Marcia is fascinating, full of interest and information from many sources. It is a story which I am familiar with, but this book has added to my knowledge with channeling from Mother Mary, Jeshua, Mary Magdalene, Martha of Bethany, Lady Diana, Archangel Michael, Joseph of Arimathea, to name some. Also, some regressions with people who remember their time with Jeshua. Added to this is much research undertaken by Marcia, but also included is her account of her trip to the Holy Land, which gave her much authenticity to all of the above. So, this is a compilation of many of these experiences.

Acknowledgements and Gratitude

By Marcia McMahon

I wish to acknowledge the late Robert Murray for contributing his part both while on the Earth plane as "Young Martha". Robert, who is in the Spirit plane where we delve in the chapters of Joseph of Arimathea who is the Spirit guide of Robert Murray. My thanks also to James Murray.

I wish to acknowledge the fine editing of Mary Mageau who put most of the book together and to Catherine Cogorno who fine-tuned the final edit.

My thanks of course to Dorothy for her graciousness and editing and publishing. I thank my friend Joanna Prentis from the UK for encouragement and commentary work on this book. I thank other friends, Dr. Laura Derr for the trip to Glastonbury and St. Michael's Mount. I thank Erica Stout, writer and contributor. I thank all the clients I've had over the years for past life hypnosis, who have contributed to this book anonymously.

Finally, I thank my Beloved Jeshua Ben Joseph, or Jesus and his beautiful wife, my sister Mary Magdalene in a previous lifetime, for their longstanding love, healing, and for the encouragement given me to go on writing even though I've lost use of my right hand.

Sincerely with great love,

Marcia McMahon

Contents

Preface

This book gathers my recollections, experiences; channeled readings and understanding accumulated over fifteen years.

I wish to clarify that some passages may at times seem discrepant with other material presented. There do still exist accounts of various past life memories, which are different for everyone. There is channeled information from Joseph of Arimathea, which is different from what I remember about Jesus in the tomb. As with all channeling, the reader's discretion is advised. Only take what resonates as truth with you and leave the rest. Even among different authors on the same subject, this happens because what we "receive" is what we need to know, or can comprehend, or what is appropriate for our learning at that particular time.

I feel that not all Truth is revealed at once, or to one person. It is an unending journey. In essence, my heart's desire is just to share beautiful teachings and enlightened mysteries I have come upon, which I believe to be of profound significance to all on the Spiritual Path, especially in this age of great awakening. And, to bring more joy and love, knowing without a doubt that our Beloved Jeshua and Mary Magdalene as well as other masters and guides are in our midst, always guiding, protecting and inspiring us. All names for past life regressions have been changed, except where the author wished to share openly, as is in my case.

Chapter 1 Message from Mother Mary and Mary Magdalene on the The Divine Feminine

Mother Mary, "I have come to speak to you today, my child, about the Divine Feminine. In my womb I bore the embodiment of the Divine Love of God. I have been many things to many cultures, and I am still revered as the Queen of Heaven. Jeshua, (Jesus) and I were part of twin souls during the early days of Earth on Lemuria. At that time, it was known as Mu, and our physical bodies contained the same soul.

"We are twin flames, and Magdalene is also part of that twin flame by her sharing a part of the Divine Goddess energy. I helped her after the crucifixion, but she had to be ushered out of Palestine in the strictest secrecy. That is part of the mystery of the incarnation—that my son had no father but the Father/ Mother God, and I also was born immaculate.

"Mary Magdalene was part of our circle of love, and we found no fault with her. Their child, my granddaughter, named Sarah, was raised far away from me. I was there at her birth in Egypt, just as Joseph and I had to flee to Egypt when Jesus was a child. Egypt is a place of shelter to all holy families and also was to be a shelter for the beautiful Princess Diana, whom you work with.

"The mystery of God and this magnificent creation does not always end up in the history books or religions, either. That is why I am larger and bigger than all the lore that is said about me. I am Mary, the Immaculate, Mother of Jeshua, and Mother of all Earth children. Come into my arms and rest from your burdens. I love you one and all with the love of the Mother."

Mary Magdalene on the Divine Feminine and her Relationship to Jeshua!

Marcia: "Dear Mary, you came to me last night in prayer and meditation. Is there anything you wish so say about your relationship with Jeshua?"

Mary Magdalene: "My child and friend, it is true of our romantic relationship. I was the woman who sat at the feet of the Master Jeshua, described in your Bible, in the house of Martha and Mary. I was the receptive one to him and I fell in love with the Master Jeshua.

"We held a friendship for many years before our romance blossomed shortly before the crucifixion. Those were both wonderful and terrible days! I gave birth to the child of Jeshua. I named her Sarah and raised her in Egypt, and then in France. Because of the persecution of all followers of Jeshua in the Roman Empire, and in 'Gaul' as France was known then, our identity was a secret to all but a select few. Sarah was my Sunshine Child and my consolation in losing the love of my life, my husband Jeshua. She provided an outlet of joy for me!

"I did write down the teachings of the Master recorded in my gospel. However, that book has been distorted by the Church fathers. I am of the Divine Feminine and I speak with compassion about the power of the Sacred Feminine. It was the mission of the Master Jeshua to bring me to leadership in our circles, which did occur with the apostles who supported me. I was later removed, and my memory denigrated to that of a harlot. Call upon me for strength, compassion and for help in childbirth.

"My Sacred Bloodline exists even today in France and England, and I leave you with this thought: history is told by the ones who control power. Look again within yourselves to the Kingdom of God/Goddess for truth! I send my love to all who hear and recognize me."

Notes:

This message dates 2005 when I began receiving messages from both Mother Mary and Mary Magdalene. It was in connection with The DaVinci Code on my radio show. It is interesting to know that the first show I did covered the topic of Mother Mary's message and Mary Magdalene. Little did I know at the time that this was the beginning of a journey into one of the most seldom-told stories of all time: that Mary Magdalene was the wife of Jesus, there was a holy child born in Egypt after which they moved to France. There was much more to this journey that was to be revealed to me!

Apparently, Mary of Bethany was important in Jeshua's life nearing the end. The Bible has stated that three Mary's were at the crucifixion. Would that then be Mary of Bethany, Mother Mary and Miriam of Tyana; or Mary Jacoby, Mother Mary's sister? I did a reading for Matiea, a friend who helped me with this first show message. She had been at the foot of the cross and was traumatized by it. I identified her as one of the holy women who watched nearby. I knew there must be more to the story, but all was yet to become clear. This was just the beginning of my quest.

Mary Magdalene of Bethany. Watercolor by Marcia McMahon. Mary self identifies as Mary of Magdalene and of Bethany. This is a portrait I channeled in and it does really resemble the Mary I knew and walked with in that past life, by Marcia McMahon

www.Masterywitharchangelmichelandmarymagdalene.com

Chapter 2 How I came to Know my Past Lives, BBS Radio, Bob Murray and Egypt

I, Marcia McMahon, have hosted the BBS Radio's Peaceful Planet show since about 2005, www.bbsradio.com/peacefulplanet.

Sometime around Christmas of 2005, I was hosting the Peaceful Planet show on Saturday evening when I had the honour of airing the late Robert Murray. He was a gifted medium and writer and a regular, frequent guest on my program. He always had very interesting things to say.

One special show I remember was around Christmas, and we were discussing Jeshua in relationship to that, when suddenly Bob began delving into my past lives, including a past life with Jeshua! I was totally flabbergasted! Choking up with tears, I listened.

With the distinct certainly that only Bob possessed, he went on. "Well you know you had a past life with Jeshua [Jesus] and I see you and the other disciples walking near Glastonbury, England, some time after the crucifixion. You do know that the crucifixion really didn't kill Jeshua, and that He survived it? I am receiving some of this information from Joseph of Arimathea, Jeshua's great uncle, who took all of you by ship to England. I've been working with Joseph for a number of years."

Stunned silence was my only response as I was totally flabbergasted, even I had recently found out that I had walked with the Master.

I replied, "Well, I've heard theories like that Bob, but I really don't remember that part while I was being regressed.

Could you please elaborate?" Still stunned, I remained silent at this profound information coming through Bob.

He continued, "I see you walking, and you had an M name. I don't think you were Mary or Mother Mary or Mary Magdalene, but you are an M name for sure. Jeshua was ahead in the group teaching there. Of course, He had to leave Israel because He was a wanted man."

As Bob said this, I suddenly put myself back there. I was left feeling as though I could follow along and put myself into the scene. I had begun to remember! "So, you feel that Jeshua did not die on the cross as has been reported in numbers of accounts in the Bible?"

Bob answered, "Jeshua would have had knowledge of how to still the heartbeat, and most likely went to spirit briefly."

I could only remember Jeshua leaving me on that terrible day, and I had been programmed to believe that as well.

Bob continued. "Jeshua had come to Britain to seek refuge. He was leading the disciples and teaching there, wandering thru the hills of Glastonbury. Jeshua had not died on the cross but knew the techniques of the yogis. He had studied how to still the heart so that He would appear to be dead. Jeshua was revived and was walking around with you in a previous life, there in England."

We delved into other topics during the interview. But I realized I needed to conduct another past life regression and find out more. Had I walked with Jeshua in England? This was all new information to me.

I was connected with another light-worker who hosted another program very similar to mine and was a gifted psychic. So, I called BBS radio. The title of her show, I believe, was *Carolyn Evers, the Messenger*. As the person on the other end was very gifted, I asked her, "Can you tell me if I had a possible past life with Jeshua in Israel?"

She took the question very slowly. I could tell that she was absorbing it. She suggested that I wait one minute until she contacted the holder of the Akashic records. Carolyn then asked me to look down at my feet and tell her if I was wearing anything. Almost instantly I saw the green hills of Galilee. When I looked down at my feet, I saw that I had a good set of sandals on. I found that I could see myself in a white garment and that it was very hot that day. Next, she led me into a meditation with Jeshua that was most remarkable.

Carolyn spoke calmly, "He is looking at you with great love in His eyes and He's saying, 'I will never leave you again'." Suddenly I'm holding His arms! I see his blue-grey eyes radiant with love and sadness. Looking into His eyes I hear the words, "I will never leave you, Martha, but where I am going you cannot go." Stunned into near silence, I managed to thank Carolyn before I hung up.

I contacted and made an appointment with a highly recommended past life regressionist, a psychologist in Illinois named Merlin. It was a unique and appropriate name for a person to perform such magic! Merlin did live up to his wonderful name!

My first regression was quite amazing, as I visited my lifetime in Egypt with Akhenaton and Nefertiti as Meritan, their daughter. Next, I saw Jeshua walking by my side on the hills of Galilee. In another regression we visited a past life with Princess Diana. She and I had been best friends in England in the mid 1800's, something the late great Robert

Murray revealed in one of my books titled *With Love from Diana, Queen of Hearts.* All who meet shall one day meet again! In one of many messages from the late Princess Diana she disclosed to me that she had been indeed the Mother of the Holy Mother Mary, and she herself had been born of a virgin.

The more knowledge flowed to me, the more I needed to know.

Other Avenues of my Early Awakenings to Past Lives Through Art History!

I taught art history for most of my life. I fell into it because art appreciation was always a course opening whenever I taught basic drawing at the college level. Usually other faculty members didn't want to do the work involved in researching all those different works of art and time periods and the history related to them. I loved it, but I had only taken a minor in art history in college and university. I always enjoyed seeing the slides bigger than life up on the screen in the large classrooms.

There were certain periods that I resonated with and always seemed to teach. It was a well-known subject in ancient Egypt that one would be teaching the Great Pyramids of Giza. I loved most of all the reformation known as Armarna period. This was an extraordinary period of abolishing pagan images and false Gods of the multi polytheistic Egyptian religion. The great Pharaoh Akhenaton arose to power and, with it, art and religions were elevated to a new understanding of the One God, Aten. I marvelled at the free flow of ideas and glorious art that flourished under this newfound freedom of worship. Thus, the Armarna period blossomed. Just looking at the statue of Nefertiti, his wife and co-regent, still gives me great pause and admiration for her beauty, and for the sculptor who sculpted her. Not to mention her status as co-regent. Egypt was the homeland of the origin of civilization, and the development of monotheism and later through Moses, who came up out of Egypt, into Judaism. In my regression, it was made clear to me that Akhenaton was my father, who later reincarnated as Moses. So, monotheism is what Moses took from his earlier incarnation as Akhenaton.

When I would present the slides larger than life on a big screen it was easy to marvel (and enter the feelings) of the royal family with Nefertiti and Akhenaton. The royal family is carved in bas relief in limestone, sitting and playing with their six children all with large heads. They are expressing great joy as the Sun God would radiate rays of the sun amongst them. It held particular joy to me, as it felt right, and somehow deeply personal.

Once while visiting the Cleveland Museum of Art with my mother, I viewed a vast cache of recently discovered artifacts from the same Egyptian period. I experienced a sudden energetic psychic realization right then and there, that I had been in another incarnation with Queen Ti, the grandmother or mother of Akhenaton. I intuitively felt that my mother had been with me in that incarnation, possibly as Queen Ti, yet I was not at that point made aware of how to retrieve past-life information. I just had an inner knowing that mother and I had been there before! It was as if time stood still and went backwards far beyond my present tense at the Cleveland Museum of Art! The little sculpture of Queen Ti was so beautifully built of clay, wood and fabric, and she was distinctly very African!

My Mother found the art works fascinating but wasn't open to discussion on whether there were past lives, which would threaten her belief system. She had been raised as a Protestant (which is clean of graven images). Oddly though, I realized in a past life regression, which I shall cover later in this chapter, who she really was and why she had an aversion to so called "graven images." Spirit told me much later that she had been a soul aspect of Queen Nefertiti.

Back to my art history lectures, I would go into a great deal of depth citing the dates approximately to 1350 BC, and the significance of it being New Kingdom Egypt. I spoke on the eminence of Akhenaton and Nefertiti and their removal of the false Gods of Amun priests. Any graven images had to go under the rule of the famous Akhenaton, the monotheist. I would always highlight the evils of the Amun priests and show how many false gods had been worshiped to a fault in Egypt. Although we all believed in the lore and the storytelling of Egypt, I felt that many of the myths that surrounded Egypt were fairy tales but knew that some were true. I personally disliked the Amun priests and their black magic.

Many historians and art historians alike cite Akhenaton as the first monotheistic ruler in the Middle East, and I tend to agree with that concept. I taught this over and over again.

The relatives of their family such as Tut Ankh Amen, the son of Akhenaton who was called Tut-ankh Aten, first, named after the new one God Aten, the sun. Of course, everyone is familiar with the famous solid gold sarcophagus of Tut. But once Akhenaton died, the Amun priests got hold of Tut by destroying his ideals and stripping away the entire heritage of the Armarna period. Another period brought the new king to his early death, and I suspect that it was foul play by the Amun priests. It is well documented in many documentary series now on the Discovery channel, that Tut likely died from the devious foul play of the Amun priests. He had suffered head wounds in a fall, but there is still speculation.

I regressed a person who remembered being Tut's queen and also his sister. She screamed in the midst of a past life regression going back to the scene as she found him lying dead in his bed from foul play.

So, this became a specialty of mine, teaching the Armarna period, as if I had been there before. And that powerful period would also come up in my side-line business of conducting regressions for people. Oddly, whenever I taught it, I attracted clients who had past lives in that period!

Another avenue of evidence for past life memories was recently found for my past life with Jeshua. Recently, I came across an old VCR tape of my family and pictures of me from the old movies they used to show on the home movie projectors from the fifties. This is another instance of toddlers remembering their past lives. In the movie I was about age two, a toddler talking about Jeshua. "Jesus had to sleep out in the rain and He had no coat, and He didn't have a place to stay!" I said it with conviction. I felt upset that Jesus had to sleep in the rain and was venting my anger. My grandfather just chuckled and thought I was so cute. This predated any religious training I had.

At that time, I had not attended Sunday school or had any religious training. Later I was to be raised a Catholic, although my mother was a Protestant.

You will find a most exciting series of regressions presented in the chapter entitled *Martha's Memories of*

Jeshua and Mary Magdalene. I also had to ask the Master Jeshua if it was so, that I was Martha. I needed to know anything about him surviving the crucifixion. So, it became a theme for me personally as well as professionally on the Peaceful Planet show, called the *Jesus Mysteries* Series.

After I asked Jeshua in prayer if I was Martha, I suddenly picked up my Bible, and there it was! When I turned to the scripture with prayer behind me, I opened the page in one of the gospels that said, "Martha had heard of Jesus and she went out to look for him and invited him to her home for supper that evening at the home of Martha and Mary." Holy Bible, New Testament.

And so I asked Jeshua directly, since I could always channel him. Momentum and curiosity made my heart pound. He answered, and His words are presented here in another message. I was on a grail quest to discover the truth. Certainly, my first show on The Da Vinci Code, on the bbsradio.com/peacefulplanet show, where for the first time I channeled both Mother Mary and Mary Magdalene, was just the start. I was on a search now for the real meaning of Mary Magdalene's life as well as Jeshua's.

References

BBS Radio.com, The Peaceful Planet show founded by Doug and Don Newsome in 2004.

www.bbsradio.com/peacefulplanet with Marcia McMahon host since 2005. We featured the *Jesus Mysteries Series*, and the *Ascension Series* every other Sat. night at 6:00 PM CST. Doug and Don are both the most open-minded light workers. My love and gratitude to them for asking me to be show host for BBS at its very beginning.

Murray, Robert. www.thestarstillshine.com,

bbsradio.com early episode from 2005. Robert channeled the *Half Beats* George and John, among other celebrities, and provided the music inspired from the other side for all these years. Now it is being continued by James Murray.

Robert passed on August 31st 2016, the same day (not year) as Diana. We collaborated on a musical project later with the late John Lennon, who is reflected in my other book, *Notes from John, Messages from Across the Universe,* published in 2012. It's an anthology of messages from the late John Lennon and George Harrison, with some of Bob's music and other music.

Chapter 3 Archangel Michael and Serapis Bey Speak on the Grand Lineage of the Divine Feminine. Channeled in the Fall, 2015

Archangel Michael: "We were present with you this evening while watching the creation of the Hubble telescope, which tells of the creation of the universe, as we know it, over universes. While it is captivating to the imagination, it only confirms that life, as you know it, is here in the present and within the multi-verse. The Milky Way is just one galaxy among millions of galaxies. So, while understanding the Ascension process of the Earth, one must also look at the cosmic implications of the millions of planets and galaxies and solar systems and black holes."

Serapis Bey, master of beauty, cosmic order and divine blueprint: "There was an ancient knowledge of the star systems in Atlantis and Egypt a long time ago. And, as well, the Holy Family began reincarnating in Egypt, for it is the home of all knowledge as we know it. Akhenaton and his queen Nefertiti were aspects of divine beauty, perfection and knowledge. Akhenaton communicated directly with the sun. Nefertiti was co-regent with Akhenaton and, as such, embodied the Divine Feminine in such an early time in Earth's history. Prior to her, of course, Isis ruled, and did so very well, even in the Atlantean times.

"Akhenaton and Nefertiti began the new religion of Aten. Akhenaton communed with the sun, as did Nefertiti, and with all of Egypt. He actually spoke with the father–Sun God. And this is no pagan rite. It is an understanding that the divine is in each and every heavenly body. And so, the predecessors of the Holy Family, which we are discussing at this retreat, existed in early times in Egypt, and prior to that in Atlantis. One might even say that the Holy Family and all holy families existed from eternity, for we all began as a divine spark, a star in the heavens, as a thought of God and a breath of God.

"From looking at the stars you can imagine the power of your sun, and how life-giving it is. You can also imagine that the power to commune with the Sun is a God-given divine right of every human being. This is why the indigenous cultures also worship the sun, because they understand its life-giving powers, even in the fires and fire ceremony.

"To honor a woman, to honor the Divine Feminine, is also very ancient and present in the Sophia literature of your Bible. Sophia existed before the Elohim and before Yahweh. Sophia is the preeminent birth figure and cosmic feminine divine.

"You might consider the Divine Feminine to be an empty container for which the Divine Masculine energy is the positive energy and the Divine Feminine is the emptiness. The emptiness needs to be filled by the Divine Masculine. The sun is masculine, while the moon is always feminine. This is not a pagan conference in any sense, as it gives you the background needed to understand the beautiful dynamics of the Divine Feminine and Divine Masculine.

"All humans have Divine Feminine and Divine Masculine parts and partnerships, whether, or not, they are aware of themselves as such. One really cannot exist without the other. Yet, oddly, one human being is a universe within himself or herself. The Divine Feminine has been called many names, Sophia being among the first, meaning wisdom. Isis was the great Goddess of Egypt, the great mother, the great mother of initiations, the great knowledge, and the mother of the resurrection of Osiris.

"Following Nefertiti, the Holy Family moved up out of Egypt and into Israel, and a new lineage was born out of the house of David. Of course, we speak of Mother Mary, Anna her mother, Anna and Joachim, and of course Joseph and Jeshua, the firstborn of Marianna. And then we speak of Mary of Bethany, Mary Magdalene, and Miriam. We speak of other characters and of other traditions. All these names carry the hallmarks of great feminine mastery. Yet, at the same time, only now are we awakening to the potential of the true Divine Feminine as that of working in partnership with the Divine Masculine.

"It is now time that the Divine Feminine must heal the planet of more war, of separation consciousness in religious ideology with male-dominated religions, in favour of compassion, nurturing love, and creativity.

"We of the spiritual hierarchy acknowledge all that you are birthing in this scared moment and we honor you today. We know who all of you are. Amen and amen. This is Lady Isis, Mother Mary, Sophia, the Master Serapis Bey and Nefertiti.

Amen

OM... Aum ..."

Chapter 4 Martha's Memories of Jeshua and Mary Magdalene

The Early Christian church of Tagba is less than one mile away from the Mount of the Beatitudes in Galilee. It radiates a sacred, early-Christian feeling. The tile on the floor and even on the side aisles of the church has loaves and fishes pictured on it. This is identified as an early Christian mosaic, much like the Roman mosaics which were used as floor coverings, initially in Roman times. The courtyard, in the style of an open-air Roman design, showcases koi fish in a lovely outdoor water garden, complete with lily pads.

Sitting in meditation I received some beautiful pictures. On the day I visited that place many memories came alive, flooding back to me. After we left the Tagba church and drove up the mountain, a magnificent vista of the azure blue Sea of Galilee appeared below, with the shrine of the Beatitudes above.

This sacred place is dedicated to Jesus, of the Beatitudes teachings. At the top of the Mountain of the Beatitudes, is a beautiful circular Catholic shrine. Inside, the Beatitudes are displayed in the round under glass, as painted by monks in the Middle Ages. Nearby is a monastery where priests continue their training. The energy of today feels just like the energy that I experienced in another life, when I had the great fortune to walk with the Master Jeshua (as Jesus' name was known then).

I will always treasure my time in Israel. It still remains a deeply sacred ground, because the Master walked there with men and women a long time ago. It feels like yesterday as I remember now, more and more. It is as though I have returned there once again. It is happening. I'm here visiting the museum and shrine, but the sunlight, the vista and the energy carry me back. I'm regressing further and further in time to that day when I walked with Jeshua upon that mountain overlooking the Sea of Galilee!

The Beatitudes, 33 A.D.

(This was my first regression session with Dr. Merlin, a hypnotherapist who led me through this with great ease. It was taken from a CD recording. Incidentals that came to mind after the session were added).

I see Jeshua in a white robe, as I am walking right beside him on a hillside. It is about 70° F and the sunshine streams all around us. He is about six feet tall with a lean frame, and he is attired in his white robe. That is the garment that he always wore. His dark brown hair gently falls over his shoulders. He walks, surrounded by crowds of people everywhere. Why am I so close to him as if I could even touch him?

He smiles, and it makes the sunshine so much brighter. His glistening white teeth and handsome looks radiate through his large grey-blue eyes. He is with us but his gaze falls far away, seemingly somewhere else at the same time.

(When he spoke or looked at you, it was as if time stood still. His eyes were deep blue-grey and penetrating, as if he could read your thoughts. Often, he demonstrated that he could do this.)

When Jeshua moves to speak he uses hand gestures. Like any teacher he must get the students' attention. He raises his hands to signal to the big crowd, which is pressing in all around us. I can see his power over the crowds, yet I cannot hear the words as he is standing in the distance now.

There is a bench set up nearby for healing. When Jeshua looks at you his eyes penetrate your entire being. One can become mesmerized by love in just one instant. He knows love, is love, and radiates unconditional love. With long dark hair and gleaming white teeth, he is what one would call very handsome, even gorgeous. He smiles frequently and, raising his hands, he gestures for those who want healing to step forth. People notice this and begin bringing the sick children.

(I baked bread that morning, and then a little boat came up and there were fishes, plus more food. I think we had unusual breads that we baked fresh that morning. We knew there would be crowds, but since we were on the road I could not possibly bake enough for a crowd that size. The little fishing boat brought about five to ten fish. They were skimpy little red things in a net. I believe it was Peter who had gone to get them, at Jeshua's request.)

Oh my, I think, that pathetic fisherman. Does he really believe he could feed this size crowd with that many fish? I ponder.

Jeshua has a special way to motivate and communicate with the people he heals. He reads the crowd, and now he is speaking. I have come to listen to him on the large hillside beside the Sea of Galilee. *This is a good place for an orator,* I think.

There are now many people herding around him. Jeshua is speaking, but I find it hard to hear him. "Blessed are the poor in spirit, for theirs is the kingdom of heaven. Blessed are they that mourn for they shall be comforted. Blessed are

they that seek after righteousness, for they shall be filled."
(These would have been the Beatitudes, of which I could
hear only a small part over the din of the crowd.)

My sister Mary and I had agreed to stay out on the road
with Jeshua for about a year to help him and to learn his
healing methods.

The day and teaching are spectacular, with clear blue
skies, perfect weather and a large crowd. We are up on a
hillside. There are mothers with their children, many with
fevers, coming toward the simple bench. He takes the little
ones gently into his arms and then touches their eyes.
Suddenly they awaken. He is healing them one by one, and
many mothers are in tears. He will take each child, gently
caress the fevered forehead, and then release that child to his
or her mother. Mothers receive their now-healed child and
respond with cries of joy, praising God. The children's
fevers are all healed within no time.

The lame are carried on stretchers. Jeshua takes his
hands and asks the evil spirit to come out of them. Many
stand up and walk. Jeshua smiles, then moves from one to
the next.

Women are weeping, down on their knees. Children
jump for joy at the sights and sounds. The lines are so long.
There are so many children who look homeless and in need.
They are in rags and have had nothing to eat. (In those days
children were not well-treated.)

I try to squeeze into the crowd to bring water to the
Master. I am afraid he is greatly tired. I see how hard he
works. He doesn't complain, just keeps going, taking the
next person. He is smiling as he works; his face brightens up
everything and everyone around him.

I was a Jew in that day and many awaited the Messiah. An older man in the crowd is loud and cynical after seeing a miracle. The reaction of some of the Jews is mocking. Right before their eyes, there is miracle after miracle. The lame walk, the fevers are gone, and they still scoff at him, call him names! The Jews just jeer and walk away.

His teachings were always the most important thing in the day, but he always healed before he taught. Mother Mary is there, sitting in the distance sending emotional support. My sister, Mary of Bethany, is close by, sending her loving support in a column of light. She has formed a kind of vortex energy in the form of the Merkaba around Jeshua. (This was a technique Mary learned in Egypt.) Some of his friends are there. I recognize Peter, James and his brother, John. I recognize Peter as a man's man. We have Lazarus, our whole group. (We planned to camp out that night on the hillside but the next thing to happen was this amazing event.)

The Loaves and Fishes

Jeshua stood up in a loud voice and thanked the Father in heaven for feeding his flock. We began to spread out little picnic blankets. Everyone pitched in. The hunger and the joy were so very palpable.

Suddenly hearts were opened, and bottled wine; caskets of wine, little cheeses and honey jars were everywhere. The fish were burning on open campfires. It was a giant picnic. Everyone helped everyone to get enough. Miraculously, there was no shortage. Not even the scrawniest of children went without at least a piece of bread in their mouths.

Jeshua created a great stir in the countryside that day. Word got out about his great gift—the blessing of the loaves and fishes. He was always working miracles, but people liked to embellish his story. The crowd made it a miracle, but it was no miracle. Everyone decided to share. He taught all day, and many would have had to journey home very hungry. I gave my bread. The basket of fish was given. Jeshua stood up in a loud voice and thanked the Father in heaven for feeding his flock. All were so satisfied with Jeshua, but in particular that day was quite special. It was the day of unforgettable miracles, both spectacular and melancholy in my memories of that past life.

This was to be one of my last days or journeys with the Master. He told me so later that day. He gently held me in His arms, I shall never forget that moment. He said, "Where I am going you cannot come, Martha. I will never leave you again." I held Jeshua in my arms, but he held me loosely. Tears filled my eyes. I could not bear to hear it. His words cut through me as giant waves of love, pain and knowing. I could not think about that then. I could not bear what the Master has just said. That entire evening, I became confused, turning within in disbelief and pain.

Eventually I fell asleep with the thought of the perfection, the glory of that day. It had been the day in my many lifetimes when I would always carry this memory within my soul. Jeshua has been my guide for many, many lifetimes, as I murmur, "In all my time here on Earth Jeshua has been my everlasting guide!"

This was my first past life regression! What a way to begin! As I reflected much later that afternoon, I wondered - had I imagined it all?

Matthew

Matthew was a dear friend in that lifetime. I looked on while he jotted something down on a parchment he carried around.

I liked Matthew; quiet and good, never minding the gossip but always a faithful follower. Others did not like him due to his past as a tax collector. All of us were Jews and all of us, including my sister Mary, had a past. Some did not like her for that past.

The Raising of Lazarus

We had a grand house. Either my father or our uncle, Joseph of Arimathea, was rich. Our home was in Bethany. It was four stories in height. This house was a mission for the poor as we expanded our hearts, also entertaining many travellers from the East. Our uncle was Joseph of Arimathea, a wealthy merchant, usually away on this and other expeditions with his great ships. And so, we had to run our giant guest house for him, as his family rightly should.

The following events happened before the final ministry we shared in Jeshua's last year. He had already left when our poor brother Lazarus died. Lazarus got sick and fell ill with fever. He died, we believed, of a fatal poison. We washed his body and had the burial and ceremony conducted by a local rabbi. In my mind I thought, this should never have happened! *Oh, if only Jeshua would have come in time, Lazarus would never have died.* But Jeshua had left us, some time before, to go about his mission of preaching and healing. My heart, my mind, my whole being called out to Jeshua, *Where were you when we needed you?* I cannot tell you exactly what he did or how he knew, but I called to Jeshua in my mind. He returned to us in four days time.

I knew I heard Jeshua's voice in my mind as he said, "I am coming right away Martha. Martha, I'm on my way! Your brother will live." *Well*, I thought, *my brother is rotting away in the tomb. What could Jeshua possibly do about this tragedy?*

We had to take care of things around the house—the olive press and the gristmill. We were not able to do these things, as we were lost without a man in the house. We could not function without our Lazarus. And I loved him very much. He was, after all, my brother, and he never married nor did I, so we were closely bonded. I bore true love for Lazarus, and Jeshua did, too.

Suddenly word came to us thru the village that the Master was on his way, and we ran out to greet him. Mary and I met Jeshua at the house entrance, and both warmly welcomed him. We then escorted him to the tomb. "Master, if you had only been near, my brother would not have died," I cried. I was in tears, but joyfully pondering his words in my mind, "Lazarus will live."

Jeshua looked at me with the gentlest of looks and said, "No Martha, it will be all right." I thought, *My God what is the Master going to do?*

I hate to tell you what happened that day, because I know you may not believe me. I indeed grieved for my brother. I was in deep sorrow as I pleaded, "Jeshua, is there anything you can do? I need my brother. I need him and love him."

Mary looked in awe as Jeshua put his hand up in the air. He made a loud cry near Lazarus's tomb. I was filled with both awe and fear. Then Jeshua cried out in a loud voice, "Lazarus, Lazarus, come out of the tomb!" To my utter horror and amazement, Lazarus appeared. He began to sit up and then pulled himself up and took one step.

My brother was in grave's clothing bound like a mummy. Mary and I were astounded as this apparition came forward. I was astonished to see our brother alive again. My heart began to pound. Mary had heard of such things in Egypt, I know, but I never ventured to ask her. Lazarus looked like a frightening sight, dead yet coming back to life! My heart pounded.

Jeshua was all smiles as he began to unwrap Lazarus, who seemed fine. His clothing was sticking to him. As we helped him unwrap Lazarus, the grave clothing did smell, but not as badly as I anticipated. No one else was available to help Lazarus. We had other old men around, but all of them were ill and too old to assist us.

Jeshua touched Lazarus again on his heart place where he could enliven his spirit. Next, we brought water for Lazarus and began to bathe him.

Mary and I were both trained as healers. We worked with herbal teas and crystals as did all the Essenes. I had to come up with things to help Lazarus feel better. Even though I was a trained herbalist I could not discover what might restore our brother. I experimented with frankincense, myrrh and teas of an exotic nature. Very weak soups were useful for him.

Mary and I took Lazarus, put him in bed and tended him. I experimented further with herbal teas to help Lazarus feel better. I stewed the herbs that I had been using to make different soups, different grains. We stayed up with him night and day. But after people have been dead, they don't suddenly jump for joy. He had suffered a bad disease. This is what took a while. I used new combinations of Mary's and my herbals. He lost a lot of weight, but with our help and over time, Lazarus was able to gradually recover his old self.

It was a true miracle. Word spread thru Bethany and people wanted to visit Lazarus. We told them the story about how Jeshua raised him from the dead. About half the people would scowl, make a face, and turn to leave the house, angrier than hornets. The Jews of that day were ignorant.

They tried to think I had turned mad or I had lost my mind, or perhaps that Jeshua had turned mad. Many Jews of that day turned away in disbelief. You have to understand what it must have been like for them to be exposed to this kind of miracle.

It made me love Jeshua all-the more. In fact, I always loved him. I knew my sister was in love with Jeshua, as well. There were many women in love with Jeshua and we were all related. Other women too needed to see him only once to fall in love with him! I held my love inside, knowing that Jeshua would only love one woman; that role belonged to Mary of Bethany, or Magdalene, as some called her.

The different Marys can be confusing. Mother Mary was Jeshua's mother. Mary Magdalene was my mother's name in that lifetime, also. Magdala was the town on the sea where my mother had come from. (It is called Migdal today, it has been excavated and found to be a fishing town at that time.) Jeshua was married to my sister, Mary of Bethany, also known as Mary Magdalene.

The Crucified Jeshua

The day they crucified him was so horrible. His brothers and sisters were terribly upset. We were all there, my sister Mary, and Mother Mary. I could see an enormous amount of suffering and torment. Blood dripped down from his head, hands and feet. He communicated with me even at a distance. To my amazement, he looked lovingly that day upon all who were crucifying him. Mother Mary stood by the cross as did my sister, making a circle around him, weeping, holding their sides with grief, and weeping more. Mother Mary knew that my sister was pregnant.

I stood at a distance, horrified. *How could they do this to our Messiah?* Our brother, John, stood by the cross, never flinching. He was lost in a world of agony, yet somewhere else.

Mary and I went to the tomb that night. I was assisting to clean and anoint the body. We put a cloth over the body. We took his clothing off. It was just horrid, as he was covered in blood. There was blood everywhere. I was not the healer for him but was merely assisting to cleanse the body. All I knew was that I anointed a dead body.

We knew the story that he would rise, of course, but were told nothing of any plot to resuscitate Jeshua. Through other sources we heard that healers came in through a secret passage, and they used a giant crystal, which was brought into the tomb. (This was my understanding later, as I did not know about the secret passage and giant crystal inside the tomb. I was not made aware of it. We were not to know about it; it was all kept very secret. To this day I am not certain of what happened to Jeshua).

Archangel Michael assisted Jesus, and I knew that angels attended him in the tomb. To me it was a sad, dark, dark day. They had crucified our beloved Messiah. I was horrified. Shock and grief were all I knew.

The Glorious Resurrection of Jeshua

In the morning, my sister Mary went to the tomb, so she could care for and anoint the body of Jeshua with frankincense and myrrh. Instead, she saw the Lord at the tomb as the angels had rolled away the stone.

Mary came home and told me everything. "I haven't ever seen anything so glorious," she said. "Jeshua didn't look the same as the old Jeshua. I barely recognized him." That made sense to me because of the severity of his wounds. I could not readily embrace this idea, and I truly thought Mary was a bit grieved and had imagined she saw an apparition of our beloved, yet she would never lie to me. I moved on questioning her.

"So, did you embrace him, Mary?"

"No, he told me not to touch him. Why would I lie to you?"

"No, Mary," I said. "I know you would not lie. I am just a bit overcome with mixed emotions right now."

Other disciples told different stories. They said he was not there, only the grave clothes. Nothing else was left behind. The angels told them, "He has been healed. He is among the living." I had no judgment about this. I was still in grief, yet a faint hope lived in my heart of hearts that our Jeshua had come back just as he said he would.

Doubting Thomas

Suddenly, I am back there again. We are gathered in the Upper Room where we had our last meal with the Master. We are in the secret room and Jeshua is showing us his crucifixion wounds. Thomas is also there.

"Just put your hands in my side, I'll show you," Jeshua said.

I felt a great deal of joy just like we used to feel. I sensed it was he, Jeshua, but it seemed as though he could appear and disappear. My concrete mind could not get those images out of my mind. I saw his dead body lying on that cloth! Seeing Jeshua alive again was magnificent. I was beside myself with joy. *What was that all about?* I was wondering what he was trying to teach us now. [Apparently, he was trying to teach us that we can do anything.] I was overjoyed. The fact that he could appear and disappear meant I might be looking at a ghost. But I do not know all the mysteries of God. I pondered this quite a lot.

It was Jeshua, all right. He could appear and reappear. I had seen the dead body as dead as dead could be. But now he was here. It was all so glorious, but all too strange for me. After everything, he had come back from the dead. Lazarus was one thing, as l had nursed him. Jeshua returned in three days, from what I will never know. He had mind power like no one else. Faith like the grain of the mustard seed, he used to say to us.

I was beside myself with happiness. I would lie awake all night wondering what he was trying to teach us now. What was his mission all about? It was too much, the fact that he could disappear like that.

Thomas did break bread with Jeshua. He doubted no more.

I don't know all the mysteries of God in this lifetime. I so admired my sister for all that she could do in that lifetime, but I was not yet ready for that level. I was just learning so much from the Master. Everything I know I learned from Jeshua and from Mary, my truest sister.

We Sail to Egypt and France

Mary and I journeyed on to Egypt so that she could deliver her baby. Our voyage was very much her hardship. I saw her pregnant on board the ship, which made her quite seasick already. I didn't like the ship because I loved our home. We were longing for the day when we could be at the fireside, telling stories, and looking forward to seeing Jeshua at our door. Now this—a seasick sister and Joseph's boat, alone, cold, and trying to cheer each other up! We all longed for home. Then we began to sing, to pass the time onboard ship.

We landed in Egypt, and Mary gave birth there, at Alexandria, a port city. Being a healer and midwife, Mother Mary supervised the birth. She knew, as I did, what to do. It was very hard for Mary being without a husband. The baby was named Sarah, said (or written) in Coptic like SARA. Mary no sooner began to nurse her than we heard a rap on our door—inspectors. We all trembled in fear. Yes, the Roman authorities heard we were related to Jeshua and the Jews. Therefore, we had to leave, immediately!

We were persecuted because we were Jews. We were called something derogatory. We were set sail on Uncle Joseph's ship, on a huge boat, for days without water. They took the oars and sails off the ship, meaning to drown us for sure. Uncle Joseph was not among us at that time, but he soon got wind of our troubles.

We may have drunk seawater; I just cannot remember how we got by. I felt the stars were guiding us, and I gazed up at them frequently to ask those out there to save us. *Jeshua, God, all our angels and lights of Heaven, our star brethren, please look down upon our ship to save us all.*

Jeshua came to us in the middle of the night, like a dim light upon the waters. It grew brighter and brighter as he appeared to be walking on the water. Luckily, we were guided to an island. We came ashore to safety; it may have been Cypress or Crete.

And so, lo and behold, we came to this island where the oars and sails were replaced. Later, we made our way to France.

Looking Back at my Life as Martha

Did I marry in that lifetime? No. I had many lovers in that lifetime. The servants told me what to take to prevent pregnancy. I was young and stupid, and I always felt that I should not have done that. This was only before I met Jeshua. After meeting him, I loved only Jeshua.

Jeshua and I worked together. But before that, I was also interested in healing. I understood the gamut of the healing herbs before I met Jeshua. But he had the healing power. None of us had that same gift. He would say that you should try all the things. He always went straight to the matter. However, I think my sister was a master healer in that lifetime. She went to the school of Isis in Egypt.

I had to make many meals for Jeshua. Jeshua's friends were not very helpful to me. To make all those types of people happy was impossible, but I did it. I was an organized person fit for the work. I remember where we stayed at other homes in Galilee. I still managed. My sister never did much work. She focused her attention and love upon Jeshua. Jeshua told me she got the better portion, and I believed him. Yet, I could not get over how my family expected me to be the cook and weave for so many. I felt that I didn't spend as much time with Jeshua as I would have liked, since I was always needed to clean things up. But I did spend one year on the road with them both. Those were my most glorious days.

Mary did sit at the foot of the master, ignoring me. Even Lazarus did not care about the home or the meals. It broke my heart, but everyone still expected me to be Martha and make all their meals.

I know there is a saying about Mary having taken the "better part" and it is so true. But where would the disciples have been without someone caring about their meals, their clothing and their care? I did the weaving, too. I don't believe they would have made it that far on empty stomachs without my small part. In fact, it is the richness of the lifetime I had with Jeshua that made the sacrifice of entertaining strangers all-the more satisfying. For this story is like no other in any of my times here on this sweet Earth.

I will always treasure my time in Israel. It is still a most sacred ground, because the Master walked there with men and women a long time ago. It feels like only yesterday as I remember now, more and more.

"Martha, my child," Jeshua said. "I am looking forward to seeing you again. Till we meet again, lo I'm always with you! Anytime you feel stressed with oppression, go back to our beautiful sessions, and imagine my energy there anytime."

Jesus by the Sea of Gallille by Marcia McMahon . c. 2003. This is actualy as I channeld Jeshua's energy in 2003 before I was regressed in hypnois or knew anyhing about the way the master looked. www.dianaspeakstotheworld.com or Marciadi2002@yahoo.com to purchase a print.

Aramaic Lord's Prayer (phonetic), as spoken by Jeshua:

To pray (in Aramaic: 'shalu') is to 'attune to', to become one with, and moved by, what is greater than our fears, doubts, and confusions!

Ah bwoon d'bwashmaya

Neeta kadasha schmach

Tay tay malkootha

Ne-whey t-savee-yanak eye kanna d'bwashmaya opfbaraha

How-lahn lachma d'soonkahnan yow-manna

Wash wo-klan how-bane eye-kanna dahp hahnan shwaken el-high-ya-bane

Oo-lah tah-lahn el-nees-yo-nah ella paewh-sahn min beesha

Metahl dih-lah-kee mal-kootha, oo-high-la, oo-teeshbohk-ta.

La-alahm, ahl-meen. Ah-mayn.

Lords' Prayer in Aramaic-
Oh, Cosmic Birther of all radiance and vibration! Soften the ground of our being
and carve out a space within us
where your Presence can abide.
Fill us with your creativity
So that we ... may be empowered
to bear the fruit of our mission.

Let each of our actions bear fruit
in accordance with our desire.
Endow us with the wisdom to produce
and share what each being needs
to grow and flourish.
Untie the tangled threads of destiny
that bind us, as we release others
from the entanglement of past mistakes.
Do not let us be seduced by that which would divert us from
our true purpose but illuminate the opportunities
of the present moment.
For you are the ground and the fruitful vision, the birth
power and the fulfillment,
as all is gathered and made whole once again.
(A translation directly from the Aramaic into English of "The
Lord's Prayer")
    for the Phonetic translation

    http://www.wayofmastery.com/pathway/the_aramaic_jesus/324
8.html

    https://www.youtube.com/watch?v=MAEIrp4MFBE

Chapter 5 Young Martha, by Bob Murray

When Martha was about fourteen years old and had just celebrated her birthday, she decided to go for a walk. This was not a usual walk for Martha, because she stayed very close to home all the time. Women did not wander away from the home courtyard. Dangers were many, and women were expected to stay home and run the house even at an early age.

Early one very hot day, in one of her reveries, Martha received a message within. Now we would call her reverie a daydream, but then it didn't have a name. Martha referred to these times as wide-awake dreaming. In her reverie she saw a man lying beside the road. Birds of prey were beginning to circle the old man. Wild dogs were moving around in the surrounding hills, and robbers had left him to die.

Martha gathered some clothing and wrapped it around herself. She didn't want her mother to know what she was going to do. She took a stone jug of olive oil and a wineskin full of water and strapped them to her waist. She left the house without telling her mother or anyone else and slipped away unseen.

Martha knew where to find the man. Within her vision she recognized the landmarks and the crossroads. She hurried on through the heat and the dust, struggling with the weight of the extra burden of clothing, water and olive oil. She saw the birds long before she saw the man. She hurried a bit faster thinking that she might be too late. She came upon

Jacob, the son of Eli, as he was about to take his last breath. She knelt down and raised the man's head. She gave him water and, as he revived, bathed his wounds with oil. "Bless you, daughter, for you have helped an old man live to see another day." With help he was able to sit up and move to the sparse shade of a tree. As Martha continued to minister to his wounds, she was wondering what to do. She couldn't bring him home with her, yet he couldn't stay beside the road. "Where were you going, father?" she asked.

"I was going to visit you, Martha."

Martha gasped and sat back. "How did you know my name? Are you from the government in Rome? You do not talk as though you are from here."

"You are to prepare yourself to be with the Master. You will become well known." Jacob swallowed more water. "I am Jacob, the son of Eli, and I was told to deliver a message to you. Yesterday I was set upon by thieves, robbed and left for dead. Today you found me and cared for me. I thank you. You must prepare yourself for a life of service."

Martha was shocked by the news. "I am but a child. I know nothing about service or about a Master, and I don't know what to do to prepare for life. What would you have me do?"

"It is not what I would have you do. I am just a messenger. At fourteen years you are a woman. You know, down deep inside you, what you must do. As time passes you will know in your heart what you must do." Jacob appeared to get weaker and was struggling to get his breath.

"Oh, please don't die. I'll get help and bring you to a house and shade." Jacob grasped her hand. "I have to leave you. Please place rocks upon my body so that the birds don't peck out my eyes." He waved a feeble hand around. "There are many rocks and only one small Jacob. Please do that for me. Please cover my body."

Martha pleaded with Jacob. "I'll get some help. I'll hurry and you'll be saved." Jacob smiled a weak smile with trembling lips said; "I am saved, daughter. I am saved." And he died in her arms.

Martha covered Jacob with the clothing after she closed his eyes. She carefully placed two flat stones over each eyelid. She spent several hours collecting stones while carefully placing them on the body. At twilight she left, arriving home after dark. Her mother was past anger, way past punishment and welcomed her daughter with open arms, just happy to see her come back.

Note:

Murray, R. *The Stars Still Shine An Afterlife Adventure* Robert's fine literary work can be found at www.thestarsstillshine.com

Chapter 6   Jeshua's Message on My Past Life

"Martha, Martha, my child. I have waited patiently to address the concerns of your mind and heart. Your mind is probing and your heart is open. You have a great combination there to do your work with spirit.

"Yes, you were in the incarnation with me as Martha. You attended to my physical needs as I travelled about Galilee and did my teaching and healing. You were a follower and, yes, it is true that you seldom spoke, as women in that day were only allowed to speak when spoken to, and not generally allowed to even accompany men in public.

"I will be fine in your sharing of your past lives at the church. In reading of these my words, I think many will benefit. There are others at the church who shared a lifetime with me as Essenes.

"Remember that I was an Essene, and that we all practiced many of the same abilities as you do today. We communed with the Father God/Goddess and we spoke with the benefit of Spirit guidance. While mine was from the Heavenly Father/Mother, others practiced what you call spirit mediumship. It may have been done secretly in our groups."

Marcia: "Can you give me any more information about the importance of that lifetime, or your lifetime that is missing from the Scriptures or has been written out of scripture?"

Jeshua: "Yes, my child, I can give you all the information of your heart. You long to know, did I have a child? Yes, I had one child, and that child is among your congregation. It is all right that they know who this child is, and that she will announce herself when she is comfortable. I was married to Mary Magdalene, and from our brief union we produced Sarah, who had been my sister Hannah. Hannah was crucified with me on that terrible day on Golgotha."

Marcia: "May I ask why some traditions say you were not crucified but instead were revived or you resurrected with your body? Can you clear this up, as my friend Bob Murray said you were taken off the cross before you died, and were revived?"

Jeshua: "Stories, my friend. I say to you, look within your heart when you saw me dying there upon the cross. This was not a position that anyone there had any choice in relieving me of. I did pass to spirit on that day. I later did reappear in a spirit formed body, and then I ascended that spirit body to a type of heavenly realm. In the higher realms I am known also as Sananda, which means the Eternal One. My ascension was complete within the forty or so days after my raising of the body. It is all true, and you may contemplate that also in the East there are records of others who resurrected the body.

"The ascended body is a little different from the physical body, and this is what all of you working on ascension will soon inhabit. It is more of a light body, filled with cells that vibrate in a different configuration.

"I did ascend, and I did many of the things the Bible speaks of. Mary Magdalene, my beloved wife, was there with me at the last supper, and so were you as you correctly remember this experience. My mother was present, and many of the male and female disciples of which you were honored to be. I am honored that you thought to ask me about the mysteries of my life and death and resurrection. Remember, too, that you had no blame in this death, and that feelings of guilt are to be released. No one, not anyone, did anything to cause it except the disciple Judas, who was programmed by his own demonic voices to betray me. On a higher level, Judas was to turn from me since he could not accept my teaching of love."

Marcia: "Thank you, Jeshua, for answering my questions. I think if I do decide to read them in church they will be quite powerful, as I know Spirit is always working to bring us greater understanding and balance in our perspectives on the scripture and real history."

Jeshua: "I am honored you called me, Martha, and I do suppose I resonate with that."

Marcia: "Was Mary Magdalene then my sister?"

Jeshua: "You have spoken well and answered your own question. I leave you my child in peace eternal. Know that much is to be revealed about these mysteries, and it will be quite a day! Enjoy the Spirit world's way of revealing secrets, and make sure you do get in touch with my lineage.

My blessings upon you all today,

Jeshua Ben Joseph/Sananda"

Chapter 7 Is Mary Magdalene also Mary of Bethany? The Mystery Unfolds

Where did the name Mary Magdalene originate? How did it come to be that there was also a Mary of Bethany, sister of Martha? Are these two historical or biblical figures the same person as Mary of Bethany claims in her channeled messages?

Mary tells me that after Jeshua left for India and married Miriam of Tyana (she was possibly a woman from Turkey whom he may have met at the well), Mary of Bethany, my sister, was in a state of total depression.

The Bible records the event in vivid detail, known as the wedding of Cana. Cana at that time was a Samaritan territory. According to differing accounts—notably *Anna, the Voice of the Magdalenes,* by Claire Heartsong—Jeshua was about to wed the woman at the well who was a Canaanite, as he fell in love with her at a very young age. According to Heartsong, Jeshua viewed this as a way to prove that love can exist between Jews and the Canaanite people. It was also an alliance, in a way, so that the family lines could be maintained. (Heartsong, cc. January 6, 2018). This wedding also resulted from a spontaneous meeting between Jeshua and the woman, who fell immediately in love with him, and thus was highly charged emotionally with very adolescent feelings. Regarding Jeshua's marriage to Miriam of Tyana (Anatolia, modern day Turkey), some accounts placed Mary Magdalene or Mary of Bethany at the well, after which she was adopted into the family of Martha. From my past life recollections and the messages I received from Jesus, I disagree.

Let us look at the Bible text to use a reference to Mary Magdalene or Mary of Bethany. In Mathew v. 28 chapter 6 it states: "After the Sabbath, at dawn on the first day, Mary Magdalene went with the other Mary to look at the tomb." Then, in chapter 5, "The angels said to the woman, 'Do not be afraid for I know you are looking for Jesus (Jeshua) who was crucified. He is not here. He has risen just as he said'." (Holy Bible, New International version.)

So, are there two Marys? Certainly, if Mary Magdalene was Jeshua's wife, she would be at the tomb to check on the body, bring frankincense and myrrh, and to mourn him. The Bible is not clear here as to whom the other Mary is. I assume that her identity remains a secret for a reason. She may have been the other wife, Miriam of Tyana, or Mother Mary. Most likely she is Mother Mary, who attended the Crucifixion as documented in John, but the other Mary is a bit more mysterious.

Claire Heartsong asserts that three Marys attended the crucifixion. They were, according to Heartsong, Mary Magdalene, Miriam of Tyana and Miriam of Mt. Carmel, the spiritual woman who never met Jeshua, but was said to be a soul mate holding the light for him as he did his ministry. This is better understood as Claire Heartsong described it in her book. She based her recollections on actual channeled material from a variety of close sources that she was able to channel. She channeled about thirty different personalities that lived with Jeshua or knew him or their descendants.

Mary of Bethany tells me that she was betrothed (meaning promised) to Jeshua at a young age. She always believed that he would be her husband. They were betrothed, or promised, at about the same age. Then, when Jeshua was travelling through Samaria, he suddenly met Miriam of Tyana at the well! He immediately fell in love and wanted to marry her.

Mary of Bethany was his equal in every way. When that event occurred, she attended the wedding and thereafter she went into a deeper depression then one can possibly imagine. She and I, as Martha, did attend the wedding but it is a mystery in the sacred writings that they were getting married. Yet, I know that Cana was a Samaritan town and the woman at the well was a Samaritan. Who, beyond Jeshua, would have the prerogative to change the water into wine at a wedding other than his own? For what would it be a symbol? It may have symbolized Jeshua's blood later at the last supper. When you are a Master, things like changing water into wine or the mundane into the sacred, are easy.

And now we enter the scene of Jeshua at the well with a woman. He reveals her past husbands and says that she can drink of the living water and never-ending life. I believe this Bible expert to be a composite, in that I don't believe any of the Marys mentioned in the Bible had multiple husbands. See John, 4:15 "Jeshua Talks with a Samaritan Woman."

When a Samaritan woman came to draw water, Jeshua said to her. "Will you give me a drink?" Again, Jeshua spoke, "If you knew the gift of God and who it is who asks that of you, you would have asked him and he would have given you living water!" Did he not tell her, about the well, that she would drink of this water and it would be the Living Waters that were everlasting life? So, the water and wine become the symbol of the wine representing the blood of Jeshua at Last Supper, as well.

Jeshua then travelled to India and left Mary's life.

Joseph of Arimathea caught word that Mary of Bethany had been staying in Magdala, a city where her mother is from, on the shore of Tiberius. Authorities are doing excavation today on Migdel (the current pronunciation). It is a fishing village near the sea of Tiberius, and in the country.

Mary went to Magdala perhaps to find her roots or gain comfort in other relationships. She told me, in her messages, that she's not proud of what she did, but she was young and in depression, while grieving the loss of Jeshua. Apparently, this is where she gained her reputation. She never sought money for what she did in her youth; therefore, was never a prostitute.

So, with much reflection and recollections from my past life there, and the evidence, and Mary's words to me, I believe this Mary of Magdala is in fact both Mary Magdalene and Mary of Bethany. Mary of Bethany was a reserved person, quiet, curious and always sitting at the Master's feet. As she was taught by Jeshua, she transformed later into a profound teacher who taught the inner way Mastery of the Divine Feminine. This comes much later in the story, so let us return to the storyline.

In *The Healing Wisdom of Mary Magdalene,* author Jack Angelo states that there is circumstantial evidence of Mary of Bethany being Mary Magdalene. "This evidence suggests that Mary of Bethany was the same person as Maryam. Indeed, the Gospel of John gives important clues in the Lazarus story. When Martha rushes indoors to her sister, she says, 'The Rabbi is calling for you!' (p. 39), she does not call him Lord or Messiah, she calls him Robonni, the affectionate name of a Rabbi." So, in the opinion of Jack

Angelo, there is the key word—Robonni—meaning master teacher and conveying a loving relationship.

Later in Mary's vision, when Jeshua appears to her at the tomb, she refers to him again as Robonni, which connotes divine love and affection.

(Author's note: When I was a child, I would sneak into my father's room and read an older Latin Missal that he owned. In the Last Super scene, the disciples were at the house of Mary and Martha in Bethany. In the scenes, Mary Magdalene is referenced as Mary of Bethany–i.e., the same person.)

Who is Mary of Magdala?

In the Mary gospel, the fragment of the Nag Hammadi found in Egypt, in about 1940, it becomes clear that that Maryam or Mary Magdalene is a leader in the new group of disciples. The writing indicates that Jeshua had a special role for Mary as a master teacher.

It has been hypothesized that her name in the Aramaic script is called Mary Master, not Magdalene. "Miriamnnae" is the Aramaic translation, according to Simcha Jacobovici, in his ground-breaking film *The Lost Tomb of Jesus*. Later, Mary's name was found on the coffin or ossuary in Israel in a scribble in Aramaic that does mean Mary Master. (Jacobovici, S.)

She has a code name in the Lost Gospel as well, not Maryam. He refers to her as Aseneth, (Jacobovici, in *The Lost Gospel: Decoding the Ancient Text that Reveals Jesus'*

Marriage to Mary the Magdalene). According to another eminent scholar, Margaret Starbird, in her book *Mary Magdalene, Bride in Exile,* she claims that the name Mary Magdalene really translates to H Magdah. And that translates to Tower. Jacobovici agrees with Starbird here. So, there is agreement that even in code—gematria—that the name has a number count of 153, which indicates a master.

Next, we look at the original text examined in the Gospel of Mary, found and written in the Coptic text from Egypt. We see a different, more mature Mary Magdalene. Mary Magdalene emerges as a scholar, teacher and Jeshua's chief disciple of the inner way of Mastery. Mary is also a visionary. After the resurrection, to which she is the first witness, she hears from Jeshua on the spiritual planes.

Evidence lies in the conversation of the disciples arguing about the authority of Mary Magdalene and Peter, who then questions her authority sharply. And thus, this becomes the turning point in Christian history—where Peter becomes the leader of the outer male hierarchy Church and Mary becomes the High Priestess of the Inner Way mastery!

High Priestess of the Inner Way is not a title that was bestowed upon Mary. Instead, she was disregarded, and her gospel distorted by even the Church fathers in Egypt, she tells me.

The Gospel of Mary Magdalene

http://gnosis.org/library/marygosp.htm

(Pages 1 to 6 of the manuscript, containing chapters 1 - 3, are lost. The extant text starts on page 7.)

Will matter then be destroyed or not?

22) The Saviour said, "All nature, all formations, all creatures exist in and with one another, and they will be resolved again into their own roots.

23) For the nature of matter is resolved into the roots of its own nature alone.

24) He who has ears to hear, let him hear."

25) Peter said to Jeshua, "Since you have explained everything to us, tell us this also: What is the sin of the world?"

26) The Saviour said, "there is no sin, but it is you who make sin when you do the things that are like the nature of adultery, which is called sin.

27) That is why the Good came into your midst, to the essence of every nature, in order to restore it to its root."

28) Then He continued and said, "That is why you become sick and die, for you are deprived of the one who can heal you.

29) He who has a mind to understand this, let him understand.

30) Matter gave birth to a passion that has no equal, which proceeded from something contrary to nature. Then there arises a disturbance in its whole body.

31) That is why I said to you, be of good courage, and if you are discouraged be encouraged in the presence of the different forms of nature.

32) He who has ears to hear, let him hear."

33) When the Blessed One had said this, he greeted them all, saying, "Peace be with you. Receive my peace unto yourselves.

34) Beware that no one leads you astray saying, 'Lo here or lo there!' For the Son of Man is within you.

35) Follow after Him!

36) Those who seek Him will find Him.

37) Go then and preach the gospel of the Kingdom.

38) Do not lay down any rules beyond what I appointed to you, and do not give a law like the lawgiver lest you be constrained by it."

39) When He said this, He departed.

Chapter 5

1) But they were grieved. They wept greatly saying, "How shall we go to the Gentiles and preach the gospel of the Kingdom of the Son of Man? If they did not spare Him, how will they spare us?"

2) Then Mary stood up, greeted them all, and said to her brethren, "Do not weep and do not grieve nor be irresolute, for His grace will be entirely with you and will protect you.

3) But rather, let us praise his greatness, for He has prepared us and made us into men."

4) When Mary said this, she turned their hearts to the good, and they began to discuss the words of the Saviour.

5) Peter said to Mary, "Sister, we know that the Saviour loved you more than the rest of women.

6) Tell us the words of the Saviour which you remember, which you know but we do not, nor have we heard them."

7) Mary answered and said, "What is hidden from you I will proclaim to you."

8) And she began to speak to them these words, "I saw the Lord in a vision, and I said to him, 'Lord I saw you today in a vision.' He answered and said to me,

9) 'Blessed are you that you did not waver at the sight of me. For where the mind is, there is the treasure.'

10) I said to him, 'Lord, how does he who sees the vision see it, through the soul or through the spirit?'

11) The Saviour answered and said, 'He does not see through the soul nor through the spirit, but the mind that is between the two, that is what sees the vision and it is [...]'"

(pages 11 - 14 are missing from the manuscript)

(The Gnostic Society library online, Jan 3, 2018 http://gnosis.org/library/marygosp.htm)

So, you see, there are many versions of Mary Magdalene. In this gospel we have fragments of Mary's words to the disciples, and her words received from Jeshua which we assume are a visionary teaching. Peter's jealousy is obvious when he says that a woman cannot accept a higher teaching than a man. It leaves us still wondering, centuries after the Nicene Council where all things were codified, for at that time it was a male dominated world.

This Gospel of Mary was considered to be radical during the time of the Nicene codification under Constantine, who Christianized the Roman world. As it was such a male dominated world at that point, no women's gospel could be considered, neither could any teachings which proclaimed Jeshua as anything other than a living God and man incarnate. Nothing but what was already decided upon could be considered! The outer Church teaching would have its way. This would become the accepted belief. There were years of debate on this theological issue about Jeshua as God and man.

Here Mary is proclaiming the inner Christ or the inner Jeshua. Also, Mary's gospel is grouped with a number of disciples who later wrote gospels, which are now considered Gnostic as in Gnosis, meaning "to know."

(https://en.wikipedia.org/wiki/Gospel_of_Mary)

(King, Karen Leigh, The Gospel of Mary of Magdala)

The Council of Nicaea brought together many of the gospels in the general codification of the bible. Nicaea is considered an important turning point in the course of history, for the codification and the canon of the teachings of Christianity. The Council accepted the first four gospels, of Matthew, Mark, Luke and then later John. And it established that Jeshua was both Son of God and human; which is not what Jeshua originally intended to teach. And then the Council established the Nicene Creed. If you haven't recited it or memorized it, you can look at the full Nicene Creed online as part of the Catholic or Protestant teaching.

Another important development of the Nicene Creed was that belief systems had to be codified into one unified message. Another belief in early Christian practice that was removed was that of reincarnation. Reincarnation, or the return of a soul aspect of a person, has been proven to be true by past life regression in young children all over the world, as well as in over four thousand well-respected studies.

Professor Ian Stevenson, the head of the psychology department, at the University of Virginia, undertook investigations. Professor Stevenson examined reincarnation and documented more than four thousand case histories of children remembering past lives. These amazing children were able to absolutely identify former places where they lived and recognize their parents by name. They provided incredibly detailed and accurate information to the researchers. Mostly toddlers we able to recall what happened in their past lives and how they died, to whom they belonged in families and even the names and address of former family members! These studies were not related to belief in reincarnation or the religion of Hinduism which is a profound belief held in the India. (Stevenson, Ian)

So, why was reincarnation removed from the Holy Bible? The answer lies in another financial and male dominated explanation, one that should not surprise us by now.

At the time Constantine was baptized, he was very wealthy. He left monuments, as churches, to the Roman Catholic Church. It was the practice then to baptize a person on their deathbed rather than to practice infant baptism as we do today. The Church could collect the wealth in death taxes with the promise of eternal life at one's death. That was how the practice of baptism by imitating Jeshua's purity came to be corrupted. As it says, "We believe in one life eternal and everlasting." The belief in heaven or hell also came about during this era, connected of course to wealth to be given to the Church for forgiveness of sins at death.

Baptism can still be practiced with sincerity, as I was re-baptised in the Jordan river on my trip to Israel, for healing purposes.

Actually, there are one or two passages remaining in the Bible where Jeshua refers to reincarnation or the characters in the story refer to the idea of reincarnation. It was popular among certain circles of the Jews at that time, especially among the Essenes, of whom we are speaking here. In Mark 6:15, the apostles or disciples ask Jesus if John the Baptist is Elijah returned or another prophet. The scripture continues, "Others said, 'It is Elijah,' while still others said, 'He is a prophet like one of the prophets of long ago'." This is one example of the belief in reincarnation. The other example is found in the healing of the man who was paralyzed who would sit by the water at Bethsaida in the temple. Some of the crowd asked Jeshua what sin did the parents commit that they should have a son born blind or paralyzed? Jeshua replied, "No sin was committed but it is to show you and these disbelievers the mercy of God and the glory of God." (Holy Bible, New Testament)

The new Canon of accepted beliefs worked so well in many ways spreading Jeshua's light and gospel of love, the forgiveness of others, his miracles and his divine truth. However, it eliminated much of the Divine Feminine mystery teachings right out of the codex of the original Holy Bible.

There were many gospels floating around then, written by many of the disciples even from the Middle East. And so, the Gnostics were totally left out of the canon of the Bible. What an incredible shame—that more than half of the known Bible was edited right out! What we have today comes only from the four synoptic gospels: Mathew, Mark, Luke and John.

Some centuries later, the monks in Egypt who revered Mary's Coptic or Gnostic gospel may have brought the Gospel of Mary with them, up from Egypt to attend the Council at Nicaea, called to order in *circa* 350 AD. They were possibly threatened with death had they stayed and included the Gospel of Philip, The Pistis Sophia and many other Gnostic Gospels available during that time period. Instead, the Church fathers of Nicaea insisted on including only the four gospels in the canon of the Bible, which formed the basis of the beliefs of the Catholic faith as it is emerged.

The Monks of the Coptic faith from Egypt would have probably been accused of heresy and suffered a martyr's death. There were many so-called heretics. They usually suffered excommunication and death at the hands of a supposedly loving Christian Church.

The Gnostic way, which Mary started, was considered to be a heresy. It developed into one of mixed beliefs, but that remains for another discussion. Gnostic comes from the word gnosis which merely means, 'to have an inner realization of the Christ consciousness.' During the last fifty years of American Christianity, this belief together with all other types of New Age beliefs, are becoming more accepted by the mainstream.

Among them are the goddess religions, which are revivals of ancient traditions which predate the Judeo-Christian traditions. New thought Christianity, such as the Unity Church, believes that the inner Christ is the one necessary component of salvation. A part of that is the belief that Christ did not die for our sins, nor was he resurrected for our sins. This theism is a more contemporary way of looking at the tragedy of the crucifixion. This teaching is a modern teaching for which the ancient male world was not ready.

I also propose that Peter had much to do with suppressing Gnostics because in this gospel you see that Peter acknowledged Mary's intimacy with and closeness to Jeshua. He grants that to her and says, "Teach us." But, later, Peter turned against Mary Magdalene. His influence became one of the prime motivating factors of all time to remove her from history, along with all that of the cardinals, popes, bishops and other powerful figureheads who become the emerging Church. Irenaeus was one of many bishops to persecute Gnostics as heretics, as well.

See: (https://en.wikipedia.org/wiki/Irenaeus)

There are many Gnostic gospels today with good scholarship to back up the entire movement that Mary began. Now, at this time in the world's history we suspect, and some know within their hearts, that Mary was married to Jeshua. As his partner, she was given to teaching others the Way, as she understood it. All of that is now exposed for the generations to examine and read. It sheds much new light on the original Jeshua movement and teachings, which is vastly different from Catholic or Orthodox Christianity. As we shall see from Mary's many channelings, she is part of the Divine Feminine energy that is grounding on the planet right now.

We cannot undo two thousand years of persecution of women such as the burning at the stake of great saints and women of strong religious persuasion. We cannot undo two thousand years of war and the burning of numbers of heretics, among them healers and women. The Roman

Catholic Church spread its teachings into the Protestant Church as there are certain tenets of the faith that are mandatory beliefs for any Christian.

The New Age includes the Gnostic beliefs, but it also encompasses all kinds of other voices and revives them as they speak through various channels throughout the world. I have channeled Athena, Goddess of war and wisdom.

Christianity claims that it is a monotheistic faith, as does its Judeo-Christian heritage. Islam is monotheistic, as well. Many of its teachings, for instance those regarding married spouses, seem to be more in line with the god/goddess concept. God is not complete without his goddess. And that is where we begin to accept the possibility that the ancients of the Hebrew Bible who wrote the name Sophia, for wisdom, knew that she was the preeminent progenitor of the race.

In Hinduism the Divine Mother is the universal and primordial cosmic energy, the one supreme Brahman, the absolute principle. She is referred to as Ma, Devi, Shakti. As Divine Feminine she takes on many powerful forms like Durga, Lakshmi, Saraswati and Parvati. In Buddhism we have several forms of Tara, with other prominent representations of Divine Feminine such as Quan Yin and Avalokiteshvara, and others.

Sophia's wisdom preceded Adam's wisdom. So, you have these ancient mysteries, some from goddess mysteries and some from the Old Hebrew Testament known as Sophia wisdom, coming to us now for a re-examination. It seems as though Mary Magdalene and Jeshua, both in the spirit realms, are looking down with a smile upon all of us. They are nodding approvingly as we open our minds to the new truths that are emerging through very ancient documents now uncovered, through channeling, and through past life regression. These are various forms of knowledge that are no longer in temples and churches and mosques.

Protestantism is waning in numbers but is still active. Catholicism is no longer thriving due to the systemic sexual abuse of thousands of children by its clergy. Aspects of the Muslim religion are flourishing among today's youth in Africa and the Middle East. Many Muslim women still wear a veil, which is a traditional sign of their faith. But wearing the burka is a way to suppress women! You cannot walk or talk in it and it's uncomfortable in hot climates. Certain forms of Islamic extremism are still promoting hatred and violent behavior. They have gone way out of line with scant respect for life and even less respect for women.

These belief systems are monotheistic in nature, and patriarchal. The one God still has a very strong male presence in the world. I feel that these structures and systems are enslaving many women the world over. I personally believe that **Mary was sent to heal the separation between men and women.** She successfully served as a wife and mother to Jeshua while he lived in his short sojourn on Earth. It is so tragic! I feel that if her story had been included in some of the gospels, events might have happened very differently in our collective history.

Collectively, we might not have had the Cathar persecutions, the Spanish Inquisition, the witch burnings all over England under Mary, Queen of Scots and the witch trials of Salem, Massachusetts. Many of these women were simply skilled as midwives and herbalists and did not practice witchcraft. Although I do not deny the existence of witchcraft or spells, I do not resonate with them. Even Wicca acknowledges the goddess traditions and the Earth religions around which the planetary and sun cycles revolve.

In the medieval times, fear was very dark. In the Middle Ages it still may have been possible to be killed in the name of Jesus Christ. St. Joan of Arc is one sad example of a talented intuitive who freed France from British rule, yet still was burned at the stake. What a tragedy this distorted religion has had upon women!

I think the male ego has something to do with why the religions cannot agree on anything. They stand in each other's light while disrespecting each other. I am not against males or the Divine Masculine qualities. I have found a few men who want to be part of the Divine Feminine and have attended my workshops on Mary Magdalene and Jeshua.

Pope Francis seems to be a shining example of a person who is willing to sit down next to a non-Christian and speak with them just like Saint Francis who used to sit down and speak to the Sultan in Egypt. Few people in our society today can appreciate differences in religion. With a few exceptions, it ends badly when people of different faiths attempt to agree or disagree or to worship together.

It is hard for us to imagine that the woman, who sat at the feet of the Master Jeshua and feasted at the house of Martha and Mary of Bethany, was, actually, the same person who was accused of adultery and almost stoned in the Bible. Yet, the sinful woman was never named. So, was it another woman?

It is easy to see why the two figures were thought to be two separate women, not one. In truth, Mary Magdalene, who anointed Jeshua's feet at the last supper, and Mary of Bethany, the quiet, meek and humble woman who always sat at the feet of the Master were the same. Mary Magdalene of Bethany was one person, the special one who witnessed the resurrection of Lazarus. Mary Magdalene was the woman with the alabaster jar, the same one who anointed Jeshua's feet before the crucifixion, and from whom the seven demons were driven out.

Now Mary entered into that fateful night at Bethany when Jeshua was reportedly at Simon, the leper's home. What leper would offer his home to Jeshua? Usually lepers were outcasts. I propose that the home the leper was living at was the home of none other than that of Martha and Mary of Bethany—the home for lepers!

On another note, in the Eastern Orthodox Church, Mary of Bethany and Martha are known as the myrrh bearers who brought myrrh to the tomb of Jeshua. Mary Magdalene is mentioned in the New Testament as being at the cross, as well as at the tomb of Joseph of Arimathea for the anointing of Jeshua.

Let us hear from Mary of Bethany as we listen with our hearts, to hear her identify as both Mary Magdalene and Mary of Bethany. From the fragments of her gospel we know she was called Magdalene, but from the geographic proximity to the Mount of Olives and Bethany we know she is also Mary of Bethany. Prepare to hear the clarity with which only holy Mary is capable of!

So, as this chapter concludes, Mary's messages shine through the sands of Egypt and mysterious encoded papyri and fragments of the Gospel of Mary. Old documents, dogmas of religion and the ravages of time shed new light as she speaks through the veil. Mary holds her lamp, as a ray of sunshine, of brilliance and clarity on the two names, the titles of honor which she holds. She speaks with clarity and a brilliance that echoes her voice in her own Gospels.

References

Jacobovici, S. Wilson, B. and *The Lost Gospel* Decoding the Ancient Text that Reveals Jesus' Marriage to Mary Magdalene, Pegasus books, N.Y.

Jacobovici, S. *The Lost Tomb*

King, Karen Leigh, The Gospel of Mary of Magdala

Starbird, M. *Mary Magdalene, Bride in Exile*

The Gospel of Mary Magdalene.

The Gnostic Society library online, Jan 3, 2018 http://gnosis.org/library/marygosp.htm)

(https://en.wikipedia.org/wiki/Gospel_of_Mary)

Stevenson, Ian. *Twenty Cases Suggestive of Reincarnation* . Reincarnation Research https://www.near-death.com/reincarnation/research/ian-stevenson.html.

Chapter 8 Mary of Bethany Reveals Miriam of Tyana

Mary said, "In those days we provided a shelter for Jeshua and his ministry. He would often need sleep and be very hungry. I spent time with him on the road, and so did you. In the last year of our ministry all three of us served the Master in Galilee.

"Martha, you will well remember our times with the ship on the sea, when it struck up a storm. Your recollection of Jeshua as being very beautiful is quite correct. Jeshua had long, dark hair, dark eyebrows, and blue-grey hazel eyes. When you looked into his eyes you could see eternity. You could see the glory of the Son of God as Messiah. I had promised myself to Jeshua in my youth. When he left with Miriam and the others in the caravan for India my heart was torn apart. I began to grieve and mope. I ceased to do the things that I used to do around the house, for our house was very diverse and we had many chores.

"I fell into what you might call a deep depression. My father at the time, Joseph of Arimathea, suggested that I go down and begin my studies at the Temple of Isis. I studied in that temple for about three years trying to put Jeshua out of my mind. It was a dangerous time for me because I was still so young and had so much sexual energy for him. I well expected that I was betrothed to him and that he would marry me. Instead, he went off to India seeking truth with the Masters."

Marcia asked, "Mary, is it true that there was another wife of Jeshua? In *Anna, the Voice of the Magdalenes* there is reference made to a Miriam of Tyana. I've been unable to contact Miriam except I thought I heard her voice last night for the first time.

"This reference is not found anywhere in the Bible. I'm really struggling on this issue, and if you could illumine my point please do. If I am not ready for the information, please move on to another topic, Mary."

Mary of Bethany replied, "Jeshua did go off in the caravan where there were other women. Jeshua was married at Cana as the bridegroom of Miriam. This is true. A streak of bitter jealousy and even other emotions that I would rather not detail ran through me the day that he was married. It was a glorious day for all of us, as I was overjoyed to see Jeshua finally happy. But, by the same token, I had promised myself to him. I felt it was my destiny and duty to be with him at least as a friend, and I had also promised my heart to him as a wife. We had known each other all our lives. You had come along a little later, but you knew him from childhood, if you can remember these images of him as a younger boy."

Marcia: "Mary, thank you for that bit of information. It is hard for me to grasp, at the moment, since I always felt that you were his only one and I never believed that Miriam was a real person."

Mary of Bethany: "My sister, it is not a thing that I am proud of—the way I behaved. But I was only a teenager at the time and teenagers behave poorly."

Marcia: "Mary, is there any truth to the idea that you had become wayward or in love with other men? Or were you remaining pure to Jeshua's heart?"

Mary of Bethany: "It is true that I rebelled and left the house for a time and lived in Magdala with my mother's people. From there, since I could not have Jeshua, I reached out to other men, you might say. I only did this out of despair for my lost love. Jeshua was my betrothed. How could he do this to me? I became confused and I took herbs in those days to prevent any pregnancy. It was made clear to me, after my father came to that household, to return home immediately and undergo the initiations in Egypt, to cleanse and purify my vessel. Joseph saved my life in that way because I would've been found in adultery, eventually.

"It is unfortunate that I have to share this part of my story. It was only later that I received forgiveness from the Master when he returned from India. He had borne three children there and he was happily married with Miriam. But when we saw each other there was a quickening of our energies again. It was not uncommon in the Middle East at that time for women to indulge in this practice, or for men to have multiple wives. Very few in the Western culture would understand it today.

"Monogamy had become the norm in the Jewish sect of the Essenes, and we believed it. But in the other Aramaic cultures around us, polygamy was still tolerated, although sometimes looked down upon. After I met Miriam, I began to love her as a sister and the jealousy faded, especially when I enjoyed meeting the children. This was a strict secret because these people would be subject to the same Roman rule, and so it was never told not even among the disciples. The disciples knew of Miriam and they knew of me, but they so looked down upon women they didn't really say much at all about Jeshua's kinfolk."

Marcia: "Was it hidden deliberately? Were there different reasons given for the children?"

Mary: "They were presented as Jeshua's sisters and their children and that is all that was said about Miriam. They eventually settled in Jerusalem and then we began our ministry. All were welcomed in this family of love, and Jeshua, being the great Master, was able to manage the difficulties of the situation. His was the purest love that I have ever known. To feel denied that love was a source of pain until I began to forgive and then reunite with all his family.

"Then, on the night he was betrayed we conceived a child, even though I was barren. To this day, I do not know how it came to be. You see that I had been barren all my life and never expected any of this. In the grief of the moment we found our love to be so true. Hence, I am not able to explain all this, but that we held a deep and abiding friendship which then blossomed into a child for us, a child that was not to know her father in the fullest sense of the word. I will speak again of our time in Bethany, Galilee, and who our other relatives were. I would be pleased to have you put this into a book, and others this year will be stepping forward to help you with both the work itself and more information. A good year awaits you, my dear sister."

Mary Magdalene in the Temple of Isis, Egypt, watercolor by Marcia McMahon. C. 2017

.

www.masterywtiharchangelmichaelandmaryMagdalene.com

Chapter 9 Mary Magdalene Speaks on Forgiveness and Her Rose

Mary Magdalene: "This is the circle of the Grail. I am the one you called Mary Magdalene. We are now interconnected as a circle of the Divine Feminine. In the sacred circle we unite in power. Many here today have done their work and have forgiven what seems to be the impossible.

"The Master used to say, 'Forgive them for they know not what they do.' And this is still true today. Your world is changing, and the Divine Feminine will finally have its way. I was an appointed apostle of the Master, and he did appoint me in charge of the mystery schools that were to go with the outer school. It is quite different now, and there will be a powerful movement of the Divine Feminine to complement the divine in every way.

"I now anoint you as part of our sacred circle. I give this to you with the rose in your heart. I am standing with Mother Mary and Princess Diana, all representatives of the Divine feminine."

Mary Magdalene continues, "I would ask you to look into Marcia's angelic Reiki sessions and her Reiki retreat. I close by sending you my love and my special rose from myself, Mother Mary and Princess Diana."

Chapter 10 Jeshua on Communion and the Royal Bloodline

Marcia: "Dear Jeshua, I was feeling that you wished to speak about your royal bloodline. Thank you for any further insight."

Jeshua: "My child, it is I, Jeshua, the Master. Happy are those who can become like children to believe in innocence without the constraints of religious dogma."

Marcia: "Dogma– the first part is dog! It's doggone gone."

Jeshua: "Pun intended, yes. Now on to my royal bloodline. Yes, there was a child, Sarah, and you are in contact with that part of her soul.

"There are other souls that share this heritage, and many in this world who carry my bloodline. When I said, 'to drink my blood,' I was giving the new covenant of Resurrection and Ascension and, therefore, the hidden meaning was to drink from my cup and become like me.

"This ritual, of communion, was intended to be an ascension activation and a cleansing for sins or mis-created thoughts and deeds. I began this during my Last Supper on Earth, though not completely.

"Communion can be practiced today with the added benefit of a DNA activation to allow for my bloodline, which includes many now, to be one in the Holy Spirit. This oneness activates the DNA and allows the monad to expand ever larger, creating a whole new person."

Marcia: "I have not seen the program yet by Simcha Jacobovici on the coffin of the family thought to belong to you,

Mary Magdalene and your other family. Can you confirm this, Jeshua?"

Jeshua, "In another message, my child. When you eat this bread and drink this cup, remember me, and there I am.

I AM WHO I AM, Jeshua, the ascended eternal one."

Chapter 11 Mary Magdalene's Message at the Chalice Well Glastonbury, UK

Mary Magdalene: "It is my pleasure to come forth and to speak to the world in this sacred place in Glastonbury—the sacred Shrine of the Holy Wells here at the Chalice Well. There is not only one Chalice Well but many wells, and the Chalice of the Holy Grail is also here, but only in spirit. For those who want the artifact, they will never find it, for artifacts decay over time, as the righteous one, Jeshua, told us all. The well is the secret place of the Holy Grail indeed! And you have amongst you many of the original disciples here today. What blessed joyous energy in union.

"Gathered around this well in memory of me we have Jeshua, and it is indeed a great day in the sun! For the sunshine is now pouring forth a magical glistening light, a rainbow. Out of the mists of Avalon on the other side of the Tor, a holy chamber is being birthed. My dear friends everywhere, this birthing chamber of the Grail child is the birth of the Divine Feminine. All the secrets that the Church has held and withheld for centuries will be known in this book and in another that will be explaining the real meaning of the Holy Grail. For the real meaning of the Holy Grail is that the grail is not a person, nor the blood of Jeshua, nor even my child. I have named her Sarah and I carried her through Egypt, then to France, and finally to England to this very site.

"The Holy Grail is not an artifact. The Grail is the Divine Feminine, which is being birthed from these wells, and from the wells of the subconscious of mankind and womankind. This is so the kindness of the Divine Feminine can be known and experienced as divine love between a man and a woman, as it was once with Jeshua and me, two thousand years ago."

Channeled at the Glastonbury Tor and Chalice well, UK 2017.

The Chalice Well, Glastonbury , UK . courtesy of Catherine Cogorno. 2016. Look at the light streaming from above also known as orbs. This place is magical.

Chapter 12 Mary Magdalene Speaks on the Grail in France

A child of the two, Jesus and Mary Magdalene, has been debated for years. In an ascension class I taught this past year, a person attending revealed a past life regression as the child Sarah, of both Mary and Jesus. More will be forthcoming as Mary would like the story told. (This has been authenticated to me in more ways since that time.)

Mary Magdelene: "My child, it is I Mary Magdalene. We spent time in France where I kept vigils to ignite the love flame for Jeshua, as he often channeled through me to help me write by candlelight at night." [I am seeing Magdalene with the crown of thorns on her head, an early Christian ritual that would be done in memory of Jeshua but not continued in ritual today.]

"I lived a simple existence in France with you at that time. We had other apostles and followers of Jeshua at that time with us, and we worked very hard on many projects. I wrote a gospel there by candlelight at night and kept it in a secret place, a kind of cave. It was known about by my knights, the Templars in the Middle Ages who re-discovered it. It may have been kept by them or may have deteriorated with time. It is not known to me, but it would be wonderful if the current keepers of my bloodline and faith, who are known today in Scotland, would be able to recognize it. [The Roslyn Chapel].

"I burned the candle at both ends being an apostle, a writer and an evangelist or carrier of the holy wisdom. We did not, at that time, call it the Grail but you, my child, are the Grail, and you are being asked to come forth with your identity and reveal the stories of our lives together in France. More regressions will be required, and you must take up the pen I left in that life and write the truth down about the Divine Feminine and the truth of the life of the Master Jeshua. Jeshua was everything to me, the heart flame of my life and the meaning of being savior and messiah. We loved one another even from beyond the grave as it is recorded in your gospels today that we met that first Easter Morning! To gaze upon the resurrection was like no other experience possible. While it is also true that I did not quite recognize Jeshua as he had gone through a transformation.

"While he did ascend in his spirit body, we were then able to communicate through my prayer and devotion to him as both my husband and my savior.

"He was and still is everything to me. My mission was accomplished, and I work from this plane now, for all who need me may turn to me and I will be there as an aspect of the Divine Feminine.

"With love and light,

"Mary of Magdalene of France of the true bloodline of Jesus Christ."

Chapter 13 Mary Magdalene's Power of the Divine Feminine and Her Rose

Mary Magdalene: "I come to you today to speak of dreams. I brought the Divine Feminine to highlight Jeshua's work in the Divine Masculine some two thousand, plus, years ago. I was His appointed apostle. The external Church was the rock—Simon Peter—and of course the inner way Church was that of the Divine Feminine. It was carried on throughout the Middle Ages through both my bloodline and the many convents that were built in my honor.

"There were other continents, other divine aspects of the feminine that were brought honor and also dignity. You know these names well: Saint Catherine, St. Therese of Avila, St. Lucia and, of course, St. Mother Mary, as in Jeshua's mother. I was also recognized in the early Church as a saint and, of course, everyone knows that saints in the western tradition are Ascended Masters in the eastern tradition. Sometimes an Ascended Master will project into another lifetime for a teaching purpose, which is what I did. This is why there are many soul aspects of myself these days. It is a grand reunion of souls at this time, is it not?

"Jeshua was concerned that the male patriarchal system would take over, and so it did. There were great efforts made through inspiration throughout the ages to bring awareness of the Divine Feminine, and my gospel was also changed by the Church fathers. You can read about it online, and you can read segments of it online, but a lot of it had decayed in the desert sands. There were others of my Gospels that I wrote in France, still buried in caves. They will be discovered at some point before the ascension of the planet. All of this is coming to light through archaeology and through past life research in order to weave a more careful garment for the Master.

"Jeshua wore a white seamless garment, and all of the Grail hunters in the world could not possibly replicate the work that we did at that time, as you well know. Jeshua encourages balance in your lifetimes, as they are dreams in a way of speaking, with the way of the Master and the perfect balance of Yin/Yang and Divine Feminine/Divine Masculine. It is not necessary to become all one or the other.

"I don't need adulation or reverence. I need a willing heart and mind to be open to my message. You, too, are gifted and this is the way that Jeshua taught. He taught love. I am forever grateful for your loving heart and kindness to the Divine Feminine power.

"I leave you with this thought: History is told by the winners. All are but dreams, yet truth is at the heart of every good dream. I am inviting all who hear me into the circle of the Magdalene Rose today. I am Mary Magdalene, keeper of the wisdom school."

Author's note:

Mary addressed the disciple Peter, whom I had regressed, and his role directly impacting Mary Magdalene's wonderful gospels and her work. She had no thought of resentment or bitterness about the treatment she received as a woman in the first century. Mary said there was nothing to forgive. Obviously, Peter didn't start the Catholic Church nor institutionalize the marginalization of women in leadership. He wasn't open to Mary's Inner Way Mastery, though, and resented her relationship to Jeshua because they were very close. Peter fulfilled his destiny beautifully, but the Church left Mary out some centuries later.

Chapter 14 Mother Mary and Magdalene Reveal the Dorset Crop Circle, May 2017

The two Marys: "My beloveds, we have stepped forth today to recognize the sacred feminine enveloped in the Vesica Piscis image located near Wiltshire, England, in May of 2017. It is Mother Mary's symbol with her image embedded in sacred geometry. As you look carefully, there is a pregnant woman encased in a pod shape, with rays of light radiating out in each direction.

"This image is also encased in the Vesica Piscis, a symbol of the fish, and is also the name for one of the gospels: the Vesica Piscis. You will also notice two very perfect orbs coming together, to represent the Sacred Masculine and the Sacred Feminine about to emerge in the solstice celebration, as well as an eclipse.

"Observe the light at the center of the forehead which serves as a reminder of my illumination. And observe the Holy Child within the womb-center as the birth of Christ and the Christ Consciousness. It is no accident that this crop circle came in 2017, with a further grounding of the energies of the Sacred Feminine. It symbolizes both Mother Mary and Mary Magdalene as holders of the sacred flame where we once lived in Glastonbury, England or "Angel Land" as it originally was called. Many of you will be exploring this very famous area known as sacred Avalon and connecting your hearts to the sacred energies that still exist there today."

Marcia: "Thank you for explaining the symbolism. Would you mind sharing how crop circles are made and who is responsible for making them?"

Mother Mary: "The crop circles are made by the collective energies of the RA group and also by the Galactic Federation as they form their Collective Consciousness into a vortex of energy that runs through the fields. They are tuned to the sacred geometry of the universe. We will continue to visit this area with many more symbols to be deciphered, and we bless you this day and remind you of the need for the Sacred Masculine to balance the Sacred Feminine in every sacred and holy relationship. It is also important to ground into the Earth with frequent visits in nature. For this is a very turbulent time, and we need each lightworker to assist us, connected to their sacred Hearts and the Heart of the Mother the Earth.

"So, as we ground these energies today let us remember what has come before and, also, rejoice at what is to come. The two orbs also symbolize the old Earth and the new Earth being formed in the womb of the mother.

"So it is. We bless you for listening today.

"We are Mother Mary and Mary Magdalene."

Reference:

www.Cropcircleconnector.org is where this image was retrieved from May 2017. Dorset U.K

Mother Mary, watercolor by Marcia McMahon

www.dianaspeakstotheworld.com

Chapter 15 Mary Magdalene Reveals the Mysteries of her Seven Chakras

The Angels: "This evening you are well prepared to channel an awesome message for now. I know you are connected to the goddess Mary Magdalene, and I feel she has something extremely important to share with you. This information includes Mary Magdalene's sacred initiation of her chakras and secret information about Jeshua, her husband and healer!"

Marcia: "I am calling upon you now as my dear sister, Mary of Bethany. I am asking for your comments on your gospel, which I am opening now and reading with great delight. Their vibrations ring so very true. You really were the master teacher, were you not?"

Mary of Bethany: "You speak well, my friend and sister. Yes, it is I, Mary Magdalene, also known as Mary of Bethany. I was appointed the chief disciple and the master of the inner way school. In my gospels you will find fragments of what was left of my teachings and the book you hold in your hands now is what was written by a fine Frenchman who knows the truth and the way and the life. [Leloup, Jean Yves. *The Gospel of Mary Magdalene*]

"Everything was deliberately kept secret by the Church fathers, and even my gospel was denigrated. But there is much truth yet to be revealed. There are just a few of you of my channels in the United States. You Martha, my sister, are a worthy channel, having worked on clearing your energy systems of any disease and, also, of any impurities. At the time of the Essenes we worked on maturity, and we worked with the chakra system as it is recorded. When it was said that Jeshua drove out the seven demons it was in reference to the seven chakras.

"It was not that I had literally seven demons, but I had accumulated karmic debris as we all do in our lifetimes. We will bring in the karmic debris from previous lifetimes plus any harm that comes to us intentionally or unintentionally in our families and our communities."

The First Chakra

"So, we shall start then with the chakra located at the base of the spine, the lowest chakra representing red. We would cleanse that chakra and then go up to the second chakra."

The Second Chakra-- Above the public bone.

"This sacral chakra was cleansed by Jeshua, when he forgave me. Then it became a vehicle for the holy child, for I was the mother of his child and the bloodline does exist to this day. In that chakra I held his seed, a new seed of life, the holy bloodline, to continue some two thousand years later.

"Many women felt attracted and drawn to the love that was Jeshua, but in this case the holy bloodline was kept as a secret. The early Church was also kept from these things except for certain disciples like Philip, yourself and Lazarus."

The Third Chakra – The Solar Plexus, near the belly button

"Next, we move up into the solar plexus, the area where we feel we can manifest our being in the surety of the light of the sun. We cleared the chakra of all cravings that are not good for us. We also cleared the chakra of any seeming self-depreciating thoughts, which of course I had."

The Heart Chakra -- the Fourth Chakra

"It is true that I was repentant when I met Jeshua on the road, after seeing him travel back from India. It is true that I was ashamed of my chakras, and so he healed me with a lightning quick fire and, further on, Jeshua ignited my **heart flame.** Once again, my great love for his blue-grey eyes, his white teeth and his open arms embraced me in that moment.

"Once again, I allowed myself to love him after I had been shuttered up in my home for years, dreaming of him but never really knowing that he would come back. All the while I was blaming the goddess Isis for my cursed state."

The Throat Chakra

"Then, as Jeshua worked with me, he gradually opened my throat chakra. It had remained silent in those days as I was never a speaker. I was not confident, but I learned confidence through him. Eventually I became quite a good teacher."

The Third Eye Chakra– Face, Lips and Eyes

"He sent healing through my throat and up through my face, and then we kissed. It was glorious after so many years of being away from Jeshua.

"We were separated when Jeshua went to India and then during the time he was with his other wife, Miriam of Tyana.

He was very much in love when he left but he realized when he came home that it was I who had possessed the inner knowledge that was to blossom. He brought it forth many times when he kissed my eyes, in hopes that they would awaken me from the nightmares that I had for so many years.

"And now, of course, he came to the third eye chakra which he awakened in a ceremony, which was private between us."

The Crown Chakra

"The crown was the head of the kundalini serpent and, as we engaged in relations, we would try to reach all the way to heaven, as if we were imagining the tips of the trees touching the sky, and it was earth and sky united in that blissful moment. And there we were, one with Father/Mother God, as he used to say.

"Jeshua had become an initiate in Egypt and, also, in India, and he had familiarized himself with the other great traditions of the day. This raising of the kundalini energy was learned in India where he studied the Sacred Tantra. For some time, I was unfamiliar with such practices and, at first, I felt ashamed.

"Jeshua, in his devotion and purity, reminded me that all the chakras can be re-energized in a moment. It happened through the pure love power we chose to emulate, so that our thoughts, our minds and our bodies would come into perfect alignment.

"When we are in the purity of love, we manifest our desires so much more quickly. This is my inner way teaching to all of you today, to work with your chakras as you heal and use the sacred energies of the kundalini for your own higher consciousness and for your own enjoyment while you are in the body.

"For healers, for you are but lovers also, I thank you for having heard my story of the Divine Feminine as an embodied disciple and wife of Master Jeshua. I am Mary Magdalene, keeper of the grail mysteries."

Reference:

Leloup, Jean Yves. The Gospel of Mary Magdalene

Chapter 16 Mary Magdalene Speaks on Her Soul Fragments

Marcia: "I am calling upon the voices of the Magdalenes—Mother Mary, Princess Diana and, if necessary, the Angels—to clarify any confusion as to why they are so many Mary Magdalenes incarnate on the planet at this time."

Mary Magdalene: "My sweet child of the light. I confirmed that it is so. I have taken on many bodies at this time, for all have a unique message of mine to share."

Marcia: "Mary, I thought you ascended with Jesus and had no need of an incarnation."

Mary: "There will always be soul fragments of myself and the blessed Mother Mary. The one whom you met on Sunday is an oversoul belonging to the soul of Isis, Mother Mary and Mary Magdalene. She has more work to do to discover her soul purpose and the details of her life so-as to place her in context to your past life."

Marcia: "May I call upon the soul of Mary of Bethany now."

Mary of Bethany: "It is I, Mary of Bethany, come to you today to illumine your troubled heart. As you know, there was more than one Mary, and we lived in harmony in the family as one. You were my sister and I was your sister. You will recall I asked you more than a year ago to get busy working on your memories with Jeshua and the storm at sea and remember his levitation."

"All that seems so impossible to your mind at-the moment, and you need not comprehend at this moment. For you are ever seeking, ever thirsty after knowledge, and for those who thirst, as the Master said, they shall be filled. I want you to rest in the knowledge that it is I in another format, in another oversoul, who visited you yesterday."

"It is true that another also carries my memories, the very one whom you work with at-the moment, the one you will be writing your book with. We have long awaited this moment of light to take place so that she could receive your training in penmanship and book writing. We ask that you involve my child Sarah into the circle of light, that her soul would be cleansed and healed enough to go on and hear the call for writing. And now that I have a fleshy body, so to speak, and she has a fleshy body, we can repair our relationship and go forth in our mission.

"All is respective of free will, of course. If my child chooses not to go or commit to your group or the Angel class, you must accept that she is feeling unworthy of the task. She is not unworthy, and you can pray for her.

"In time, another will also step forth and write her version of her memory of Jeshua. For she shares your memories as you share hers, and it will be a grander soul reunion than you can possibly imagine at-the moment. Mother Mary is guiding your group the entire way, and it would be wonderful to honor her by holding her rosary during your sessions."

Marcia: "You know I don't pray the rosary. Are you asking me to simply hold it to connect to Mary's vibration?"

Mary Magdalene: "Yes, we just ask you to hold the vibration and continue to say a prayer on the rosary once in a while, especially for your dear mother who is not well."

Marcia: "That much I certainly can do, and I will call my mother right now."

Mary Magdalene: "We of the spiritual hierarchy and I Mary of Bethany, also known as Mary Magdalene, come to you this very day. Rejoice in the knowledge that you have; and be not confounded by who was who and what was what. Your analytical mind will be satisfied, and all will be happy with the result of the knowledge. I bless you with my light and my pen. We hope you can use your channels to bless and not to confound. I leave you to ponder the mysteries of Jeshua and the Magdalenes."

Chapter 17 Mother Mary Shares her Words of Wisdom in a Special Message

Mother Mary: "I am the one known as Mother Mary, and I come this day with joy, knowing my children are happy and healthy. I bless each one of you with my rose and, of course, if you like to say it, the rosary. I know that most of you are Catholics, and some of you are not, and it matters not to me for I am larger than all religions. And I speak through many masters on the Earth plane, as all have different messages from me, the Higher Self of Mary who bore Jeshua and brought him to you through my earthly body.

"Many of you belong to the greater soul family of Mary and Jeshua, and the Essenes, as they were called back then. And so, my dear friends, this is a soul family reunion. And there are many more awaiting the knowledge that Marcia has shared, and others have shared in your private circles."

"I am one of the highest examples of the Divine Feminine, and it is my greatest pleasure to give you a divine spark, in essence of myself, through the rose oil or the rose water from the Chalice Well."

"This special water and oil have been blessed just for you for your healing today and, whether you are male or female, you may receive it and receive a cleansing."

"I bless you all and want you to know that I work with Princess Diana in my healing circles, as well as Mary Magdalene. We are all three here together celebrating in the higher realms, and we ask especially that you pray for peace, especially in the Ukraine and for Russia.

"We see in the next few months there will be turbulence in that area, and we ask that you send the world peace meditation out to that area and the areas of Africa and also the Middle East. So many people are suffering the world over, and I tend to appear in the most desperate of places in order to give my loving comfort as a mother to all peoples. I am still, as Diana is, mother to many who have no mother. If you feel so moved, please donate to Marcia's Healing and Peace Center, which will be temporarily housed here at Stillpoint, as I see it.

"I bless you all and I love you all. You are welcome into the circle of the Divine Feminine and my Rose.

"With love,

"Mother Mary, Mother of Jeshua"

Author note:

This message about the Ukraine was channeled in 2014 and sometime later in 2014 there was the downed airline over the Ukraine, MH17 Three Russians and one Ukrainian are being prosecuted for that terrible crime. www.bbc.com

Chapter 18 Lady Aurora Speaks on the Divine Feminine

Lady Aurora: "This is Lady Aurora. I am the Divine Feminine energy, and I come with the greatest love, awe and respect for the Creator.

"I am the creative intelligence of the Cosmic Mother, the birther of all radiance and vibration!

"I embrace you this day with the arms of the Divine Feminine. I held many names throughout the ages, as Shekinah and Isis, Mother Mary, Mary Magdalene, and many more in ancient cultures. I am the Mother to all of you, my people of Earth, and the Universal Mother in the Heavens. I am robed in purest white and gold cloth.

"I dwell in the secret place of the Most High. I am who I am. I am the Alpha and the Omega. I am the dance and I am Shiva, the dancer. I pulsate with life energy, and I am the still waters of the soul.

"I am crying out to be heard in this society which pollutes the Earth and denigrates women in false teachings. I yearn to become one with my peoples. I and the Father God are one, and yet my cries for my people go unheard. My children are dying, the Earth is in upheavals, I yearn for my waters to be free and my people everywhere to have joy.

"I am the sound of the waves upon a beach, and I am still waters. Blessed be all who hear my pleas for my people, to make peace, and let my children all go free. Listen to my call and hearken to the call of the mother, calling you home.

"Rest in my truth today for I am comfort.

"I bless you.

"I am Lady Aurora."

Lady Aurora by Marcia McMahon, watercolor 2016

Available at <u>Marciadi2002@yahoo.com</u>

Chapter 19 On the Road with Jeshua and Mary Magdalene, A Regression with Angela

Marcia: "You are becoming so relaxed, so very relaxed, and the tips of your toes and your muscles are all relaxing now. Let this relaxation flow into your feet, your thighs, your waist. In a few moments, I will be taking you on a trip into a lifetime that you lived long ago, an important lifetime or lifetimes. And you are going deeper and deeper. Twice as heavy. A guiding light of the angels is all around you, and that is the presence of God and the divine. This beautiful white light will keep you safe should you encounter any difficulty as you re-experience this lifetime where you lived before. Now go on relaxing. More and more deep relaxation encompasses you. You will remember everything you need including things that are very important. You will be able to speak, and you will now remember everything perfectly.

"You are standing at the top of a heavy staircase. Feel the carpet below you. With each step down you feel deeper and deeper relaxed into hypnosis. There is door on the beach at the end of your staircase. Across the beach is a door. The door of time is up ahead on the beach. It is standing ajar. Go ahead. It is just as you left it the last time you were here on the beach of never-ending life.

"Go ahead and open the door for yourself.

"As you approach the door of time, you are ready to enter the past. When I count to three and say go, you will enter the past. One two three and go!

"Where are you what are you wearing? Where are you? Who are you with?"

Angela speaks as Mary of Bethany. "I looked down and I'm wearing sandals and a white tunic with a blue overcoat. We're carrying some things—some healing herbs and some crystals and some little baskets. It's a special day out on the road in Galilee with Jeshua. We're going about healing in remote villages that are what you would call today quarantined. The leper colonies have been cut off from normal society. I feel that we are with a leper here."

Marcia: "Okay, so tell me more about what happens after you enter the village."

Mary: "The sun is shining brightly and beautifully, and we all feel so in love today. I'm in love with Jeshua. We're all in a loving community of healers. There would be about five of us on the road. I feel that you, Martha, are with us also.

"We approach this one hut-shaped building. We knock before entering. We enter and it's just a very humble place—almost nothing. People have almost no food, nowhere to sleep and they're very desperate for healing.

"Jeshua and I are primarily working energy healing on this old man; he has a cane and he's very, very old and he's somewhat deformed, as well. We're giving him relief although we're not restoring him. You are assisting with giving water. Everyone works on him and he begins to smile. There begins to appear a twinkle in his eye. It's also very touching. I begin to cry. I'm so overwhelmed with this simple love he emanates."

Marcia: "What happens next, Mary?"

Mary: "We go to another hut where there is a family of people living there again. There's almost nothing inside. It's made of stone plus some grass for the roof. It's out in Galilee somewhere. The people are so thankful to see that the Master, Jeshua, has come. They are also in need of healing. There is an elderly woman there who needs help. She's been afflicted with the disease for a long time, but the others in the family have chosen to stay with her.

"We perform our healing on this elderly woman who was very frail. She has rags for clothing and the people in the house are also very poor. They offer us lunch and we agree to stay for lunch. The woman puts a fire together and makes us some unleavened bread. She also offers hummus and olives and whatever they have. They don't have much, but they give everything that they have in the home in gratitude for the healing of this older woman. The older woman is able to sit up, now, but she is very weak and will take some time for her healing. In cases of leprosy often all that could be done is to use energy healing. Often people could not be completely restored.

"We are weeping silently for them. They have given all they have to use for their lunch. I am so touched. He [Jeshua] and I are so happy together. We share what we brought in our little picnic baskets, and all are filled."

Marcia: "Mary, can you tell me what we learned from Jeshua of his healing methods? How were we trained in healing?"

Mary of Bethany: "You and I were trained in herbs and crystals. This we learned at home from our mother, Mary of Magdala. Well, I also studied at the Temple of Isis in Egypt. There was more healing included. Also included in my studies was the study of the resurrection of the body, the dying of cells and the renewing of the Life Force to the cells.

Jeshua was also trained in the Resurrection temples in Egypt and he also trained in India."

Marcia: "Mary can you explain what happened when you were sent down to Egypt by Uncle Joseph, or father, into the temple to study at the Temple of Isis in Egypt? I heard some pretty strange things about that."

Mary: "I am there now, and I am seeing myself in a line of young women being in line to be initiated by the Great Mother Isis. We studied at the temple for about two years there. During that time, we learned many healing techniques and we also learned how to please our husbands. You would call it today chakra or tantra training. We learned the Arts of the Mysteries of the Divine Feminine. We each were initiated in our cycle of the moon in a ceremony. Mother Mary led us with a white rose and a red rose. The red symbolized the flowing of blood now that we are young women. The white symbolized the male energies. We were taught the ways of sexual energies and how to ignite the kundalini energies between male and female.

"We studied and practiced with healing oils such as frankincense and myrrh, which were widely available for embalming in Egypt. We experimented with gold palladium, also known as gold emporium.

"We had daily rituals of bathing. Then we had the ritual of Resurrection, or of the laying inside the coffin of the great Pyramid of Cheops or Khufu. This was thought to be the biggest test. And for me, unfortunately, it left me in a bad state-of-affairs.

"I can't breathe. I see that Jeshua is coming. He says he's coming to me. I know he's in India right now with Miriam of Tyana, but Jesus is coming to me to rescue me! I'm nearly suffocated. They put the top of the coffin on as part of our final initiation. And I-I'm dying! I can't breathe. I'm barely alive." [The lady, presently under hypnosis as a soul aspect of Mary Magdalene, has to get her nebulizer and have a breathing treatment.]

Marcia: I administer Reiki and Healing—hands-on healing energy work to Mary while she struggles with her breathing and her nebulizer. When she's recovered enough, we go back to the regression to find out what happened.

(Author note: While under hypnosis, physical ailments that are the root cause of symptoms in past lives may come up. The regressionist needs to be skilled when the physical symptoms may arise. Most regressionists would not continue the session.

Apparently, while in Egypt, Mary went very deeply into a trance in which she was oxygen deprived and she nearly died. This was common among the Mysteries in Egypt, and particularly in the mysteries of Lady Isis. It was believed that if you were worthy of the initiation you would put all your cells to sleep and—quote, unquote—"die". Then, given time, you would know when the right time to "wake up" was. It would increase your longevity.)

Marcia: "Are you all right now, Mary, and shall we go on?"

Mary: "Yes, I'm quite all right. Thank you for administering your healing intentions.

"In Egypt we also learned to harness the energy of the sun. The great sun god RA was part of our initiations. We learned to lie in the sun and absorb the sun's energy in, to such a degree that we could use that extra energy absorbed and stored in the etheric body, for hands-on healing. So that's why Reiki energy, as you call it today, was so powerful. It was because we harnessed a marvellous tool—the tool of the sun—for healing. We also had sets of crystals that we used for sound healing and chiming. We would use chimes that were available, such as gongs and cymbals, but also rattles and different things that we wore on our wristbands.

"Every initiate had a snake or a symbol of Isis on her wristband. Both upper and lower arms were covered in gold bangles and bands. We also had scarves and were taught how to dance—to sway, much like your belly dance today—so that we could be pleasing to the man.

"We did not practice with men. We were only taught the practices. Since we were Jews, we were very guarded about our heritage, and many people did not distinguish us from other Egyptians studying in the school of Isis.

"But we were particularly aware of the power of the kundalini energy and our sexual energies. Mother Mary had come to the temple once when I was there as well. Mother Mary was also known as the high initiate in the school of Isis, but she was in the school of motherhood, not in the school of kundalini."

Marcia: "Do go on, Mary. You were saying something about Jeshua coming to you while you were trapped inside a coffin at the Sphinx or at the Great Pyramid of Khufu."

Mary: "It is true that at the very last moment of breath [in that coffin rite of passage] that Jeshua appeared in my mind and he said: 'Mary, I love you and I've always loved you. We will meet again!' And he breathed just a breath into my lungs, there in the tomb. Someone heard a rustling noise of me crying for help. The lid was lifted off the coffin. I was allowed to come out, but I wasn't the same. I was told that I had been in a long trance. My body had grown cold and I could have nearly died. It was something I don't remember. I only remember people are telling me what happened and what I looked like. I could not speak, neither could I eat.

"I was sent home immediately because I was in a deep trance and they couldn't bring me out of it. The trance lasted for about a year or more, as you will remember. At that time, it wasn't understood that it was a form of spell or mental illness.

"This was thought to be a high initiation, but in fact it was a dangerous practice. A call was put out to Joseph of Arimathea who came on the ship. Joseph was infuriated when he found me in this condition. He brought me from Egypt back home to Bethany where I could be nursed back to health.

"At that time this was a misunderstood initiation. Although I respected the school of Isis greatly, I came to question why Mother Isis would leave me barren. I noticed that I no longer had my monthly cycles, either. At that point I decided that I would devote more time to healing myself and learning the lessons we were provided in Egypt, as well as healing others at the home in Bethany where we ran the orphanage. You'll remember, Martha, that we did not have the tools that we have today for depression or for severe shock. I was in severe shock for more than a year. During that time, you tended me. I could barely speak. If it was not for Jeshua coming to me at that moment inside the coffin I would not have been able to live at all."

In Early Egypt 3000 BC, Angela's Other Memories Surface

Mary: "I'm further and further back in the nation of Egypt."

Marcia: "Where are you, Mary? Look down at your shoes and tell me if you are male or female and what you're wearing."

Mary: "I am wearing a beautiful breastplate. It has the feathers, the lapis lazuli, and the pure gold of the Mother Isis. My name is Isis in this lifetime, and I am with my husband Osiris on his throne. We were ruling over both Lower and Upper Egypt in this ancient time."

Marcia: "What is your husband's name in Egypt?"

Mary/Isis: "Of course he is Osiris, the Great One. He is my current husband in this lifetime. There was an evil plot to take over our reign. People were at a party. They stayed over twenty hours and emerged drunk, to plot to kill my beloved. They sliced him into many pieces and put him in the River Nile. In my determination, I gathered the pieces together and reassembled him. I did the ritual of the healing of the sun with a large crystal, utilizing the sun's energy. To be exact, I resurrected Osiris. He was incomplete, but complete enough to revive him."

Marcia: "And then, what happened?"

Mary/Isis: "In the brief time that we were together on the Earth plane, before Osiris ascended into the heavens, I became pregnant. I don't know whether it was a light infused pregnancy or natural pregnancy. He died shortly thereafter, of course, suffering from those wounds. But then I gave birth to Horus."

Marcia: "Just go on now and tell me the rest of the story."

Mary/Isis: "Many people regard the story as total myth, but there is some truth to it. I did give birth mysteriously. My son grew and he took over all of Egypt once again. He is known throughout the land as the Falcon Bird. He is a symbol of our resurrection practices that were only known in the secret temples, hidden away in the temples of ancient Egypt for centuries. It is now time for this message to be heard.

"For worship purposes, this is the worship of the Goddess. The goddess predates the idea of the God-being. Goddess must give birth to God and not the other way around. She is the primal genitor of the species. She was worshipped in all our cultures. And so, the ritual of Isis and the healing of the sun with the use of the crystals were also done to Master Jeshua.

"This lifetime was very important for my understanding. At the time that I studied in the school of Isis I did not know that I was a soul aspect of Mother Isis. Mother Mary and I, as well as others of our group, and the Essenes, were initiates into the Isis Magic. This has all been hidden knowledge, but it is being rediscovered in crystal healing today. Also, it was used in Atlantis times very long ago.

"So, when you ask how we did the healing, on that day we used the energies of the Sun and we had our crystals. We were actually calling upon the Mother Goddess as much as the Father God. This is not known in your Bible because the patriarchs of the Church have taken it out. Jeshua understood that holding the Sun's energy inside the body would impart great healing to those in need. And so, I end my story in a simple way. The buried knowledge in the school of Isis needs to come forth more and more, so her ways are more understood. The ways of Isis are mentioned in your Book of Genesis where we speak of her as Sofia. Never forget that the Mother is the source of all. The mother is the more important one because she gives the life and she holds the key to life and death. And so, it is that Jeshua helped me out of that, too. We reunited back in my home at Bethany some years later."

Marcia: "Amazing, isn't it?"

Mary: "It is known in the Egyptian legends, but it has been distorted. I tell you that the goddess is progenitor and co-creator. One cannot be without the other. And so, it is we learned these practices and we adhere to the Goddess Isis.

"When I came back to Bethany, I was in such a state of depression that I came to pay the price for my barrenness.

"But for this, we shall wait for another time."

Marcia: "Thank you, Mary, for sharing this school of Isis and the practices of her school. I am glad you are aware of the Goddess energy being brought back from the tomb today, as many are awakening now to the Goddess energies and a system of thought that makes so much sense."

Author's note:

Isis has nothing to do with the current Middle Eastern terrorist group, nor would it be related at all. If you look up Egyptian symbols you will always find Lady Isis.

Mary in the school of Isis by Marcia McMahon c. 2018

Marciadi2002@yahoo.com for prints

Chapter 20 Mary and Jeshua Still Heal Today from the Inner Planes. Miracles are Available for All!

Marcia: "Dear Mary Magdalene, I was wondering if you could describe your knowledge of healing techniques and what you did with your healing skills throughout the Galilean Ministry and then into your life in Egypt and France? And, I wonder if you would recommend a specific healing technique for all of us. You described the healing that Jeshua gave you for casting out the seven demons. Did he actually cast out demons?"

Mary Magdalene: "Thank you for asking this question, my Sweet Child of the Light. Yes, Jeshua was a gifted healer and he knew how to go straight to the source of the problem whether it was physical, emotional, epilepsy or some form of demonic possession.

"We usually called it demonic possession, but it was mental illness at that time. There were sometimes Spirit attachments or things of that nature. Once I was cleared, and my chakras felt whole again, he began to work with me and teach me how to perform different types of healing for different types of emotional needs.

"What I understood was that a lot of the root cause of the illness was often a person's past, and usually they felt violated by something. Perhaps violent things that happened or they were rejected, or they were afflicted with a rare type of an illness such as leprosy, or even cancer. Often, they held a thought of being unlovable or unloving toward oneself or another. And these unloving self-deprecating thoughts would accumulate and sometimes form an illness.

"Or, there were people who were perfectly healthy who would contract a sudden illness which, at that time, we believed to be a poison. That could also be known in your culture as a virus. When we worked with the lepers, we extended our heart of compassion. We were not afraid to lay hands on them to do energy work.

"This was seen as a very suspicious activity when the priests found out about it. But, you see, the people were deteriorating rapidly from their disease. It would have looked horrible and tortured them. Usually none of our healers would get sick because we believed in bathing and washing of the hands. But we also practiced a form of spiritual protection by actively surrounding our selves in the light of the angels, calling upon our personal Angelic and ascended Master groups, before we would do that type of work. With Jeshua, he made even the most awful situations into ones of mercy and great joy. He was also an exorcist in the strictest sense of the word.

"At that time, in the ancient world, things like depression or manic depression where people would get mania and were lashing out at other people like a lion, was considered a demonic possession at that time. People were often suffering from depression as well as spirit oppression and repression of various thoughts. Jeshua could see the spirit that was oppressing the person and trying to kill the person, and he could command that spirit to leave immediately.

"Very often these spirits would roam about looking for another person and then possess them. So the story of the man with the demon possessed and then the demons were sent out into the pigs is true. I was there with him at that time.

"The person who wanted to be healed had to have faith that they would be healed. The faith that they would invest in Jeshua was great because he had a wonderful reputation as a Healer. It was almost as if it was miraculous, but the faith and lack of self-doubt suspended even for a moment would allow the total healing, the total miracle of a person to be released. Then the Master would say, 'Go and sin no more, or tell no one!' That was because people were thinking or feeling wrong.

"His fame in the Galilee region became so great that he became very much pressed upon to perform miracles all the time. He did his miracle healing in the beginning of the session with the groups, and then he would move into the teaching, which was far more important. Since I was his primary student, I would learn how to do the healing and the teaching with him.

"I could see, and I could learn to see into the person's mind what the illness was originating from. Mostly there were emotional issues attached to illnesses, but some were, definitely, inherited. And some were completely demonic, while others exhibited a form of mental disease. Very few times in his life did he not heal, but I do recall that in his hometown he would not be able to heal or teach. And so goes the saying 'the prophet is never given honor in his home land'.

"Jeshua is with all of you who are reading this who are in need of a healing, and I am standing with him. You can invite us in as a team and ask us to cleanse any chakra that you know you carry, be it shame or that you know you need an emotional, physical or mental healing. We will do it from the Spirit planes. We are always here for you, my dear sister. You have been through quite a lot of illness in your lifetime.

Anytime you feel a need for the cleansing of your chakras you can let us know and we will be glad to come to do a session.

"You can rely on us, and all of those reading my message today can rely on us to do a healing for you. Time does not matter, but space does in the eternal moment of now and the healing of the relationship—the emotional core issue relating to the illness—and, of course, the setting right of the DNA. All of this was done in just a moment, and it can be done if you have enough faith. But you must hold faith and dissolve fear and doubt, for fear brings with it many forms of illness.

"I leave you in blessed peace today, my sister, and I ask you to continue to ask for your healing whenever you need to. And that goes for all the readers of this most wonderful of my sayings. For I am still healing from the inner planes and am still working with women and men to balance the Divine Feminine Masculine.

"I am Mary Magdalene, the healer and partner of Jeshua. May miracles be with you, my sister."

Author's note:

I found this particular message from Mary Magdalene to be so beautiful. I could feel her and Jeshua's presence with me. As I have still carried the tendency in my soul to worry. I've gone thru stage four cancer and I am now healed. I do have periods of self-doubt, depression and anxiety. She explains how one must release the illness and thoughts about it and have complete faith in miracles! www.masterywitharchangelmichaelandmarymagdalen.com

Chapter 21 The Garden Tomb of the Resurrection of Jesus in Jerusalem, and other Tombs of Jesus in Afghanistan

I have yet to connect all the dots on this mystery of Jesus' life, death and his many surviving tombs. However, the name Essenes pertains to the Jewish sect we belonged to. Miriam must have been someone I had met briefly in my past life as Martha before Jeshua left for India. Then, Miriam dropped out of the picture and retired from Jeshua's life during the Galilean ministry. Possibly Miriam was rumored to be living in Jerusalem.

Certainly, I believe that there were three Marys at the cross—Mother Mary, Mary Magdalene, and possibly Miriam of Tyana or Mary Jacoby. Some feel that Mary Jacoby was a name made-up by the Catholic Church in order to cover for the fact of there being more Marys at the cross than they could account for. She is also thought to be Mother Mary's sister. I know I was there, too, but I felt that I was at a distinct distance. I looked upon Jeshua upon that cross from a distance, as for some reason I felt that I was being held back for my safety. Apparently, Mary of Bethany, or Mary Magdalene was important in his life nearing the end and that is well recorded in the Bible.

I did a reading for a Matiea, a friend whom I identified as one of the holy women, possibly Mary Jacoby or one of the Marys at the cross. Of that I was sure. Matiea had a fear of being a light worker, due to–witnessing Jeshua's terrible pain and suffering that day. That would scare anyone!

Martha's memories surface now. I was standing too far off to do anything but watch the horror unfold. I was

115

devastated and the family was devastated. I witnessed Jeshua die on that cross notwithstanding the naysayer who says he never died. I spoke to him in the Spirit realms that sad day. He said, "I am fine now, Martha." He smiled, and I saw him in his white robe just as he had been before all this nightmare stuff began. I blamed the Romans. I did not remember even the faintest hint of resurrection in that first regression.

In another book, *Anna, The Voice of the Magdalenes* by Claire Heartsong, she details that Miriam of Tyana was at the cross along with Mary Magdalene, as well as Mother Mary.

In the account of *Power of the Magdalene* by Joanna Prentis and Stuart Wilson, we also see that the three Marys were there. There would have been Mother Mary, Mary Magdalene and Miriam of Tyana. Joanna and Stuart have since reappeared on my Peaceful Planet show on (www.bbsradio.com/peacefulplanet) and reconciled the feeling that my original channeling from Mary of Bethany about Mary Magdalene being identical with Mary Bethany was correct. She was one and same person.

My feeling is that there were many holy women around Jeshua, and most of them had a Mary name. I still cannot totally recall the existence of Miriam of Tyana. I have channeled her. She has come through for me, so I know she did exist. As far as my memories, I only remember Jeshua being married to Mary of Bethany, my sister. That doesn't mean that settles everything. Very often in past life regressions we are given only a certain amount of knowledge at that particular time. The memories are continuous, so we can find out more. They last but a short while and we cannot absorb the information in one session.

Past life regression, like channeling, is oftentimes told with a particular perspective. I don't believe that channeling is inaccurate, nor do I believe that past life regression is inherently inaccurate. However, like any story, some will see a different perspective of a past life depending on who the main character is. Sometimes there is distortion on the part of the person under hypnosis, but I have not found that. Some people can retrieve only some details. They may need more than one regression. I have regressed two Mary Magdalene subjects. Could they both be telling the truth?

Inaccuracies, of course, can occur with these intuitive journeys. Very often I've been in a past life regression and come home to do research on what I saw and found that the facts verified rather than contradicted what was experienced in that lifetime.

Once, at a psychic fair I met another person from the same general geographical area. Archangel Michael told me she was a miracle worker and I thought that I should get to know her. I did a reading for her, and she was confirmed as being a soul aspect of Mary Magdalene. The earlier painting that I have made of Mary Magdalene looked similar if not identical to this lady.

I participated in a group regression in which this particular lady remembered being in India with Jeshua and offered descriptions of visiting different temples. She also remembered that we were together in the burial chamber at the Garden Tomb of the Resurrection in Israel. She mentioned that when she anointed the body, she felt a slight pulse. That also adds to the intrigue of the story.

In the final analysis, I rely upon Mary Magdalene in Spirit because I'm primarily a channel for Spirit. I have found over time that my messages from Mary Magdalene are entirely truthful. However, I am sure of one thing, past life regression is not a factual experience of anyone's lifetime. But it can be relied upon when facts back up the experience. As Mary always likes to say in her messages, "History is told by the winners!" And it is true that Mary Magdalene's gospel was all but blotted out by the Church fathers and Constantine in 350 AD. Therefore, the only way we have of knowing what may have really happened with the life of Jeshua and Mary is through past life regression, archaeology, new progressive research and channeling, plus her existing gospels which are readily available online, known as The Gospel of Mary.

In the book *Power of the Magdalene* by Joanna Prentis and Stuart Wilson, it is also made clear that there were people placed strategically throughout Jerusalem to hold light and healing energy for Jeshua on that day, and to heal him and to send light for the column of the Cross, so that he would not die completely. There were crystals that were placed around this very site, and a powerful crystal was set inside Joseph's Garden tomb. There are purportedly more than three to four supposed tombs of Jeshua Ben Joseph or Jesus Christ.

A famous Jewish archaeologist, Simcha Jacobovici, living today, teaches and claims that he found the actual tombs of Jesus, Joseph, Mother Mary, Mary Magdalene and quite a few children belonging to Jesus in Jerusalem buried underneath a suburban apartment building as ossuaries, in Jerusalem. This shook up the Protestant and Catholic scholars quite a bit!

The Israeli authorities explored this tomb for a brief time in the seventies. Components were removed for study at the

Anglo-Israeli Archaeological Society, as the ossuaries were removed. Jacobovici wrote an entire book and made an entire film concerning this explosive material.

Jacobovici writes that he found the cache tomb relics of Jesus' whole entire family. The ossuaries were dated to the first century by carbon 14. Their names were Mary Magdalene, Jeshua son of Joseph, Mary, Jose, James, and others. I have seen ossuaries too, when I was in Israel, near the Garden Tomb. They were moved into an Israeli museum, and Jacobovici produced his first very controversial film about the tomb of Jesus. One can imagine the uproar this film caused in the traditional Catholic and Protestant churches and the Jewish community in Israel. They did everything to debunk it!

This particular tomb of Jeshua and his family had a chevron as the symbol of their graves. It was in a suburb of today's Jerusalem. It was explored, dug, excavated, and the items of the grave plot were saved for further inspection. Then the fascinating grave was covered over by a modern Israeli apartment building. This is shared in Jacobovici's film titled the *The Lost Tomb of Jesus*. It would explain the second family theory, of Miriam of Tyana, since neither Mary Magdalene nor Martha would be buried in Jerusalem. It is possible that Mother Mary and Joseph would have had their family ossuary's there, too. But it appears they are not buried there!

In that day, some people were buried in that common style, in ossuaries. Now it all makes sense. The ossuaries of Jeshua contained his wife, possibly Miriam of Tyana and 3-4 children, if you believe that theory. Since Miriam of Tyana was said to live in Jerusalem, that would place those tombs there. I'm still unsure how to understand Miriam of Tyana, other than what Mary Magdalene has revealed to me.

I expect that no bones were found in Jeshua's tomb. When I asked Jeshua about this, with my usual curiosity, he replied he would respond in another message. That was intriguing but not conclusive.

Jacobovici caused quite a stir! Is it possible that this was the alternate tomb with the three children rumored to have been born to Miriam of Tyana? There is a tomb with an inscription in Aramaic for the word Mary that says Mary Master, or tower as Simcha translates it. As well, there are three children or ossuaries for the children. Which of the ossuaries contain actual bones? I'm not really sure.

Every Christian since childhood many have been told that Jeshua died for our sins, and then was raised from the dead on the third day. This business of other tombs would call into question a great deal of orthodoxy concerning the core teaching of Christianity. This states that Christ died, and then was raised from the dead by God, the Father alone. If any bones were found in the Jeshua ossuaries, it would strike a blow to the commonly held beliefs of most Christians. That is why Simcha Jacobovici has not been popular among any of the religious leaders or theologians. His suggestion threatens Judaism, it threatens people's belief systems, and even crossed the line with Protestants.

Strangely, all the biblical scholars started accusing Jacobovici of being a total fraud. I wonder why he was considered a fraud. Was it because they could lose their seats of positions at universities as professors? Or were they affiliated with the Vatican? The official stance from all Church authorities would be, "Don't let truth get in the way of our dogma." And Jeshua told me himself, dogma is dog gone! The Vatican would never endorse this because it doesn't fit with their model of so-called Christianity or Catholicism. To whom could the family tomb belong to, if not to Jeshua and his family? The names were all there. Obviously, it was controversial.

I wanted to know if that was the original family of Jeshua and whether the children would have been his or Mother Mary's. There were Jude, Jose, and another girl's name inscribed on the ossuaries. Additionally, there is far more to the story. Did Jesus possibly survive crucifixion, or did he die temporarily and was possibly revived by Joseph, Mother Mary and perhaps Mary Magdalene?

The Garden Tomb of the Resurrection in Jerusalem

I have visited the Protestant Garden Tomb of the Resurrection in Jerusalem. It was a spectacular sight to behold and contained a miraculous energy vibration. As a psychic, that divine energy said it all for me. The Garden Tomb is located about a half or quarter mile away from the Damascus gate of Old Jerusalem, and past the Garden of Gethsemane. First you have to walk through the Garden of Gethsemane before arriving at the Garden Tomb. A small entrance fee is charged or you can make a donation. It is run entirely by volunteers from England belonging to a Protestant non-denominational non-profit group.

Not only was the Garden tomb spectacular to behold, with its large size and well-manicured gardens, but there was also Joseph of Arimathea's winepress a few feet away from the door to the tomb. Behind the rock cut tomb was Joseph's original home in Jerusalem. The orbs of light were everywhere, another energy signature!

So, the story really fits with the rock-cut Protestant tomb outside the walls on the Damascus Gate near the Garden of Gethsemane. The rock-cut tomb garden was definitely the marking point of Jeshua's burial and resurrection.

I could feel the energy and the memories return to me. Not only was the tomb beautifully spectacular, the rock cut tomb and garden well kept, but it had beautiful and significant signs around the garden identifying Joseph's wine press, the hill of Golgotha, which was a few hundred feet away! There was the huge wheel shaped stone (now missing but carved into the tomb wall behind it), which was rolled outward to allow visitors to gaze upon the spectral chamber where once the Divine Master Jeshua had laid his body down. The sorrow I felt upon looking inward at the chamber where he really lay made my heartache.

The huge, wheel shaped stone carved Roman arch, now around the outer perimeter of the matrix of the tomb that had been rolled away was there! It met every description of a large, perhaps 30-40 ft high stone, that fits into a carefully carved grooved water trough, so-as to roll. This is described similarly in the Bible as having been being rolled away by the Angels when Jeshua was found not to be in it. There it was!

Marcia McMahon

The Garden Tomb, Jerusalem

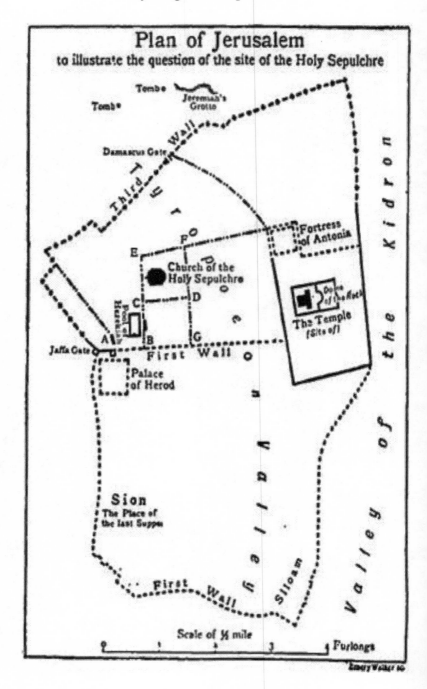

Note:

This illustration is from a map of Old Jerusalem, and the Garden Tomb is located outside the walls and near the place of the skull known as Golgotha.

https://en.wikipedia.org/wiki/The_Garden_Tomb

The Damascus Gate is the same road as the Way of the Cross (Via Dolorosa). Is this another archaeological coincidence? I think not. I walked out the Damascus gate that day to see and behold the beautiful Garden tomb of the Resurrection! It was a half-mile away on the same road as the Via Dolorosa.

The energy of the Garden Tomb's surrounding was heavenly, the orbs appeared everywhere, surrounding various vistas and people; even the plants emitted this vibrating energy. Stepping inside the tomb, all is clearly identified through the many places mentioned in the gospels. The facts speak so clearly here, that so much of this place belonging to Joseph of Arimathea did make sense archaeologically and technically speaking.

The most interesting and spectacular thing of all to happen when I stepped into the tomb was that I remembered the way Jeshua had lain as we wrapped him in linen clothes and placed him in the grave. I recall that he lay facing the Damascus gate.

My brother Jim looked around for the tour guide and asked, "Where would the body of Jesus have fit into this small tomb?" I immediately called it to mind and answered him. "He would have lain from this way to this way against the wall." Not long afterward, the tour guide from another Protestant group came in and explained that the way I had identified was exactly how his body would have been placed in the tomb. My brother Jim looked up at me with a curious look on his face. He has heard my Martha regression, but he is a practicing Catholic, so I surprised him there.

We stayed in the Protestant Tomb of the Resurrection Garden most of the morning. I caught a lot of orbs on film around my brother and his friend as they read the resurrection account when Mary came to the tomb early in the morning on the third day. It was a like a confirmation. Again, the energy was so vibrant and alive in that spectacular Garden! The Garden tomb features lilies and geraniums and exotic Middle Eastern trees. (Wikipedia, Garden Tomb, scholars state that Skull Hill and the Garden Tomb are located in close proximity to the Damascus road, about 200 m. from Damascus Gate.)

It felt very much like the true tomb of Jeshua. Truly, it has all the names and places associated with the crucifixion and archaeological evidence, also. The other tomb of Jesus is called the Church of the Holy Sepulchre, including an underground tomb in the middle of Jerusalem, was not even identified until ca. 350 AD, by Constantine's mother, Saint Helena. She had a vision where the tomb of Jeshua lay, and began a dig there in 350 AD. She proclaimed a few relics to be the genuine cross of Jesus to be located there. Thus, the place was made famous, considered sacred ground and a great church was built there. But it doesn't correspond to scriptures at all, and old wood is found everywhere in ancient Israel or Palestine as it was called in her time. I am not discrediting St. Helena, as I am fond of her for bringing in so much light to the subject of Jeshua. She converted her son, Constantine the Great, to Christianity. This allowed the Romans to bring in the new Way. The faith, even if in a distorted form, was important to many more millions. She herself, although pure, came from a corrupted family filled with intrigues of Constantine's many disturbing deeds. He was largely responsible for eliminating the teachings of Mary Magdalene's Gospel and removing the belief of reincarnation, as it was understood in the Middle East and the ancient world.

In my personal regressions and memories of Jeshua I do not remember him being tended to in the tomb, except that we all did the washing and anointing; nor do I recall any plan of such a nature. I was Martha, a practical Jewish woman concerned with cleanliness, orderliness and proper burial procedure. I was not aware of anything like the possible revival of Jeshua.

I present this material because I've been exploring it for many years and there is overwhelming archaeological evidence to support the idea that Jeshua may have survived the crucifixion or been resurrected. From there, Jeshua possibly continued all the way through India up into the Himalayas in Nepal, where he stayed briefly at the Himmis monastery, wrote another book, then possibly ended up in Afghanistan, where there is a tomb dedicated to Issa, the Healer of the Lepers. Issa is an exact translation of the name of Jesus in Hebrew. So, how do you explain that tomb away?

Did Jeshua Die on the Cross, or was He Revived? More Tomb Questions

In his message to me Jeshua made it quite clear that he did die, then he did experience the resurrection. But what was that Resurrection? Was it actually through the healers who came into the tomb and revived him with crystals, as is written in *Power of the Magdalene*? Did Jeshua simply still his heart and temporarily go to Spirit and come back? Or, was he revived from near death, as Bob Murray and Ed Martin have said, based on both psychic and archaeological research?

It was odd and good timing that I interviewed Joanna Prentis and Stuart Wilson authors of the *Power of the Magdalene* one week, and then the following week, in May 2009, I interviewed Ed Martin of the *Jesus, King of Travelers, Jesus' Lost Years in India* film. They all said the same thing, that Jeshua possibly survived the crucifixion. Ed Martin said there is a tomb in Afghanistan to this day housing Issa, Son of God and Healer of the Lepers! I was astounded by the theory that Jeshua did not die on the cross, however, now I consider that a real possibility.

The claim that Joseph of Arimathea was aware of the plan to revive Jesus after being taken down from the cross is a theory that supposedly Mary Magdalene and Mother Mary knew. All three worked with distance healing. Purportedly, there was a secret entrance to the tomb, designed by Joseph from behind his house, whereby healers would enter and administer aloe, myrrh and other healing balms to Jeshua's wounds. While there, I viewed no such secret entrance or backdoor trap door, whatsoever. I looked about carefully while in the rock-hewn Garden Tomb, and the rock was seamless—no evidence of any lines in the rock or anything. I felt the walls; they were cold, no trap door anywhere. Also, upon looking at the rock-hewn tomb I saw nothing that even remotely suggested a secret entrance other than the giant stone that had been rolled away. Of course, I realize that it has been two-thousand years and something could have been changed. Yet, this tomb did have Joseph's wine press right outside the door of the tomb. No doubt in my mind, this was the rock-cut tomb described in the Bible.

As Martha, I can now remember him coming and going in his resurrected body, looking just like the Jeshua we knew, and acting just like him. But then he would suddenly disappear. It took me a few sessions of regressions to get that far, as upon my first regression I had no recollection of Jeshua after death.

On the other hand, in the regression of John the Beloved disciple, he remembers that Jeshua's resurrection was totally physical. Mary confirmed she saw him but did not recognize him. Apparently, in the story revealed here of Mary Magdalene she experiences him differently in the Spirit light-body. So, how could she have possibly been to the tomb secretly to heal him? Gospels are always missing pieces and facts, and in Mary's own account of the Resurrection, in this book, she said she could not touch him. So that implies light-body.

The story became even more intriguing when I interviewed the now-famous Ed Martin and his filmmaker, Paul Davids. Introduced together on the Peaceful Planet show, Ed Martin claims that he visited Afghanistan in the Peace Corps in the seventies. While having a beer at the PO he noticed that it was called Murray Beer, and he asked why the name was Murray beer? The bartender explained, "No, sire! That name Murray means Mary, as in Mary the mother of Jesus!" He told Ed that Mother Mary's tomb was right around the area and so was Jeshua's ancient tomb! This was when Ed was in Afghanistan.

You can see the film, *Jesus in India*, by Ed Martin and his filmmaker Paul Davids. Read the book, *Jesus, King of Travellers* as I highly recommend it! This is a different account—an Eastern tradition of Jeshua walking back, post crucifixion, on the silk road by camel and by foot, progressing through India and the Himalayas, finally arriving in Lhasa at the monastery high in the Himalayan hills where he supposedly lived and wrote. His code name was Issa, Healer of the Lepers. There is a tomb surviving today known as "Issa, Healer of the Lepers"! Carved over the tomb of Issa (Jesus in Arabic) lays peacefully the body and sculpture of this figure. It has crucifixion marks in the hands and feet.

The person had been crucified and then this carving over the body is precisely first century, roughly corresponding to the same era as Jeshua.

Ed Martin is a very honest and thorough researcher. He has a psychic gift, as well, but his book is based on factual research only.

Ed followed the show I did with Joanna Prentis and Stuart Wilson on *Power of the Magdalene*, when both claimed that Jesus never died but was gradually healed with the use of crystals and herbs, and that He was taken to Damascus and then healed. He eventually headed into the Far East on the Silk Road to continue his journey of bringing truth to the people there.

In another book, *Divine Union*, author Lea Chapin remembers her past life as Elizabeth (cousin of Jeshua) who with Mary Magdalene tended Jeshua's wounds after the crucifixion and revived him in a secret cave that Joseph of

Arimathea had arranged for him. This book, too, details that Jeshua eventually travelled to parts of India in his ascended body form.

Certainly, the authors of well-researched material such as Ed Martin, a researcher and traveller, as well as Jacobovici, author and researcher, didn't make this up! Gifted psychics, Akashic readings, past life memories have presented themselves now for this reason: to ask what really happened to the Messiah Jesus, and did he, as lost records indicate, possibly survive the Crucifixion? Did he carry forth his beautiful message of healing and love to India and finally pass away in Afghanistan, as most Muslims in that area of the world believe? Did he study with the Masters of the East and have secret knowledge from the great Mahavatar Babaji? There are many tombs of Jesus, all in different areas of now Israel, and then one strange one in Afghanistan. I like to think that these mysteries remain as evidence for a reason and are surfacing now for us to re-examine the "Good Old Story of the Cross."

Was Jeshua ben Joseph a world teacher of religions or just a messenger to Israel? I like to think of him as a great Master and Master Teacher of World religions, a bringer of hope, love and truth, a transcendent master of death, a world teacher! By all indications his influence was far reaching in his day, and the Christian story needs amending to include all his travels to India be they astral, physical, or Ascended. His beautiful bride Mary Magdalene needs to be included as the greatest disciple! The mysteries will continue to unfold provided that archaeological evidence isn't suppressed, and the psychic revelations will continue to be presented to the public.

References

Cannon, D. *Jesus and the Essenes.* Published by Ozark Mountain Publishing www.ozarkmountainpublishing.com, 1999

Chapin, L. Divine Union, *The Love Story of Jesus and Mary Magdalene.* 2017.

Davids, P. Jesus in India the Movie. Jesus-in_India_the_Movie.com 2009.

The Gospel of Mary. http://gnosis.org/library/marygosp.htm

The Gospel of Mary Magdalene is part of the gnostic gospels.

The Garden Tomb of the Resurrection, Jerusalem https://en.wikipedia.org/wiki/The_Garden_Tomb the carbon 14 dating of this tomb dates back to the early 4th or 5th century.

Jacobavici , Simcha. *The Lost Tomb of Jesus.*

Jacobavici, Wilson, Barry. *The Lost Gospel, Decoding the Ancient Text* that reveals Jesus' Marriage to Mary Magdalene

Heartsong, C. & Clemett, C.A. *Anna Voices of the Magdalenes, A Sequel to Anna, Grandmother of Jesus*, 2004. Hay House, Carlsbad, www.hayhouse.com

Martin, E. *Jesus King of Travellers*, Jonah Press, 2007

Ozark Mt. Publishing, AK, USA

Prentis, Joanna, Wilson, S. *The Power of the Magdalene.* 2009

Chapter 22 Archangel Michael Speaks on the Ley Lines, Stonehenge and Sacred Sites, as well as Crop Circles!

Archangel Michael: "Yes, it is I, Archangel Michael, and you felt my loving energies as you traveled southward from Avebury and Bath down through all the sacred site energy, all the way to the tip of Cornwall known as Archangel Michael's Mount. Yes, Felicity does anchor the grid with her crystal and grid of pink rose crystals and, yes, I, of course, was with you two. Actually, my energy and ley-line were upward toward the Mount of Saint Michael. You will recognize the feeling of the energy as you've been in Cornwall before in other lifetimes; and, as well, Felicity anchors quite a good amount of Jeshua's energy. You connected to this as well as to Mother Mary. We are delighted that you've made some new contacts in the United Kingdom and renewed some old friendships. I was guiding you and Joanna all the way up to the Tor, and I assure you that it was my energy that brought you forth as you were too exhausted in the physical vehicle to be doing it on your own!

"I wish to thank Johanna for her energy of joy and adding that burst of energy to bring you forth to the Tor. I wish to also thank Laura and her energy, confidence and joy as she, with you, traveled around the sacred sites of England. Everyone's energy was welcomed and received by myself with great joy, love and understanding. Everyone's need was met in a perfect way, and the sites that you saw were perceived as ones of great beauty and magnificence.

"Now, I will connect later on the powerful ley lines and how they relate to the crop circles, and what is really going on here on a metaphysical level. I wish you to rest a while and then come back for the remainder of the reading. I'll even leave you in peace, my beloved.

"Continuing then to address your question, it is I, Archangel Michael! The Ancients always knew about the ley lines and tended to build their stone circles around powerful energy spots, which could be felt in the human auric field. Think of a ley line as a meridian point on the grid of the Earth. There are a great many grids and ley lines present in southern England, all the way from one tip to the other, and as you were traveling, you were following the Michael ley line, laying down the magnetic pull to Mara Zion and St Michael's Mount

"When you reached the end point, you felt the bliss of the Mary line intersecting the Michael line. Moving on then to your direct question about the relationship of the crop circles, to the ley lines and to early Stonehenge, you can see that they are based on sacred geometry and the movement of the stars, in many cases. The magnificent creations of sacred geometry that do manifest in the fields are from both angelic and intergalactic fifth dimensional collective beings of light. Some would call them Pleaidian, some would call them Arcturian, some would call them the Elohim or the RA group. The mystery of the creation is imprinted in a single grain of sand as well as in the pictures of the Milky Way galaxy.

"And, intermittently, we have visitors from off-planet in a collective cloud of vastly phenomenal intelligence, which does create and generate the geometric perfection of the pi ratio and patterns of unspeakable beauty and symbolism.

"Each person should look to the various crop circles to determine the genuineness and the message for themselves.

In the case of the airplane or bird shaped crop circle near Cornwall delivered May 4th to a place very near St. Michael's Mount, these visitors were busily creating a type of ship. I would say to you to look that up on a crop circle connector site.

"Marcia feels that it represents a jet and the travels of the lightworkers to the sacred site and pilgrimages being made to England and her holy sites. I confirm that I am and was present with Marcia on the entire trip, as I was with her friends as well. I am present this evening anchoring my energy and shedding light on the program, Peaceful Planet Show, as well as on this world.

"We look forward into the grandest event of all, the Ascension, which is to be in the next few years. There will be more signs embedded in your crop circles, and we encourage lightworkers to pray for one another's safety as we all travel to the various sacred sites and meridian points of this sacred Earth before her Ascension.

"I leave you in peace and blessings, and I ask that all pray for World Peace at this time, for there is a great tension and many storms and, of course, all of this is detailed in Marcia's precious book, *Ascension Teachings with Archangel Michael.* As well, there is a dangerous situation brewing in North and South Korea, and we ask all lightworkers and peace workers to pray for a peaceful settlement. We, of the angelic realm and the Intergalactic Federation of Light, will do all we can to prevent that catastrophe to Earth at this time. We thank all our listeners.

"I am Archangel Michael, and I bid you peace."

References

www.cropcircleconnector.com,

Ascension Teachings with Archangel Michael by Marcia McMahon, 2013 on amazon.com.

www.MasterywithArchangelMichaelandMaryMagadalene.com

Chapter 23 Simon Peter's Regression, by Lydia

Note: Lydia remembers her previous life as the Disciple Peter. The time is after the crucifixion and resurrection.

Lydia: "I had my session with Marcia yesterday. Like my email communications with her, it felt so easy and natural, like having a conversation with a friend.

"The first image is a black pole out in the water, tipping slightly to the right, with something attached to it near the top, perhaps an iron ring. It is an offshore anchorage for a boat. The air is foggy, it is early morning. Then I am on a boat, my boat. I don't want to be on shore, there are awful things back there. I want to escape, go back to my peaceful life as a fisherman, have nothing to do with all that. I am on my boat because it is familiar and comforting. There are other men with me including my brother Andrew. He is quiet, but my support. I rely on his care, he admires me, and we are a team.

"We are all feeling discouraged—no fish. I'm watching the daylight increase. There is a tall, slender man on the shore. As he talks to us about fishing—we are not far out— I'm starting to get a feeling of familiarity. I look closer and see it is the Master. I can see his face clearly, those beautiful eyes that look right through you with the purest love. Love! When I feel that love, I throw myself into the water, weeping. I am a very passionate man. I don't care that my robes are wet and binding around my leg. I only want to get to him for he is alive—my Master whom I'd felt so helpless to save!

"I throw myself at his feet. He lifts me up. I think he uses words, but mostly I just *know* what he's telling me. By asking me, 'Do you love me more than you love fishing' he is guiding me to *feel* the Love that I experienced in my relationship with him and to bring me back to knowing this experience is true. It has not been lost through the trauma of the crucifixion. He wishes to remind me to live in this Love, not to run away to my old life of being a fisherman.

"All this is conveyed in a flash. He knows I wanted to run away, to find solace in my previous, simple life on the lake. But I am forever changed. Experiencing the purity of God's Love through Jeshua is not something I can wish away. He asks me again, do I love him, and then again. He is leading me to my own experience of my love. It is something *I* experience. It did not die with Jeshua, nor is it something he alone has. By telling me to feed his flock, I am learning that by sharing the love—giving it away—I will multiply its power. This is far more important than fishing and feeding my own family.

"He is also conveying his confidence in me. He is performing an energy transmission, attuning me to his vibration of love so that knowing truth can carry me through my mission of bringing his energy into the world. It's not just his teachings and the stories about him, it's his energy. Writing this now, I realize how totally irrelevant are Peter's and my current fears about being unworthy. Jeshua had no resonance with that thought. He did not even acknowledge or engage it. He chose me because I chose him. I am part of the Team, the plan to bring Light to the world, to wake humanity up! This is all that matters, not some paltry thought of unworthiness.

"At the end of reviewing this life, Marcia asks what I now understand about it, from the perspective of after-death. I see the Earth covered with a thick blanket of something like a layer of dense fog. Each point where I performed the miracle of healing creates an opening where the Light is anchored onto the Earth. I can see the energy exchanging as shafts of light—a pathway between the living waters of Earth and the loving fire of Heaven.

"Also, I see that Jeshua, Mary Magdalene and the others opened an enormous portal of Light in Jerusalem—an ecstatic explosion that forced back the powers of darkness, forever weakening their grip. All of us working to bring openings for the Light are weakening its grip, making more and more holes until the veil of darkness dissolves, like pulling apart a soap bubble membrane or a sheet of silly putty.

"Marcia brings me forward. I can feel myself teaching. I have always had a way with words, but now, when I attune to my Love for Jeshua, beautiful, confident words about his love for all of us, and God's love, come pouring forth. People whose languages I do not speak understand me. I feel very humble. Clearly this is not 'me' speaking. It is through no education or skill of my own. (But I see now, writing this, that this humility was, in part, Peter's feeling of unworthiness. He always said, 'It is the Master who uses my hands, my voice. But now I see that I am his equal. As a Soul, I am equally loved by God, my willingness allows the love of God to pour through.' I can feel Jeshua saying, Yes!! and laughing as I write this.)

"I can see myself on the Island of Crete, in the shade of a beautiful tree, with my traveling companions—three men and a woman—performing healings. I call on Jeshua's name, bringing in his love and power. Laying my hands on where the person has pain, I feel the heat and light and energy come through my hands, as my body experiences the person's pain, drawing it off of them and down into the Earth. My body and the patient's body form an electrical circuit to join the living waters of the Mother and the loving fires of the light of the Father. It is amazing. I have no idea how this is working. I praise Jeshua. I tell people, 'See his power? This is why you should believe in him.' My companions support me with their love, their belief in Jeshua, and their devotion to him.

"There are times I can feel his presence, and times not. I miss him. I weep and feel despair. And then I continue on with my healing and preaching his love for all.

"Marcia progresses me forward, wanting me to go to another happy experience, but Rome keeps drawing my attention. I don't like Rome; it is loud, dirty, busy, uncaring, selfish and egotistical in the extreme. I am concerned about Paul, distressed that he is under house arrest. I am in a safe house, a wealthy Roman house with an atrium and a fountain and arched walkways. People in my community (I realize I've been here for quite some time, preaching and healing) are trying to convince me to stay away from the Roman authorities, as there is nothing I can do to help Paul. But I am stubborn. I feel that I failed to prevent the death of John the Baptist in prison, I failed to prevent Jeshua's death, so I'm not going to give up trying to prevent Paul's death.

"I go to a large building with white steps. The guards laugh at me and push me away. I feel pathetic, an older Jewish man, bald on the top with a curly white beard. I am nothing to them, amusing. I persist. I am imprisoned in a dark place, I feel despair, not believing that my work has made any difference. I abandoned my family, and all for what? To have failed, yet again, in saving a friend?

"Here is where Marcia comes in and says, 'We know how it ended.' She asks how do I see the value and purpose of this lifetime? As Martha, her admiration of me (as Peter) is very helpful to hear, to counteract Peter's despair, and the depression I am currently feeling. I do see that Peter's service in passionately conveying Jeshua's love, and demonstrating it with healings, was extraordinarily important in encouraging the light of love to shine in the mind of humanity."

McMahon, M. *Enlightened Hypnosis*

www.enlightenedhypnosis.net

Chapter 24 A Past Life Regression of Hannah and Sarah written by Erica Stout in Her Own Words 7/21/2017

"I went under past life regression with a professional regressionist by the name of Merlin (aka Doc). I do not recall the exact date of the regression, but I do remember it. As I began to relax and Merlin was slowly directing me into a trance, I saw myself in a large theatre-film room as if I was to review a film. It was like they do in the industry, but instead of a film like a movie, it was of my past life. In the trance, I sat down in this room and, as the film began, I saw that I was in a foreign land. It was sandy, and I was with a man who walked beside me. Merlin then began to ask questions, as follows:

Merlin: Where are you?

Ericka: I'm walking on a dirt road and I see a valley below me.

Merlin: Are you a man or woman?

Ericka: I'm a girl.

Merlin: How old are you, and what is your name?

Ericka: I don't know how old I am, but I am a girl of a young age.

Merlin: Do you know your name?

Ericka: Hannah.

Merlin: What are you wearing?

Ericka: I'm wearing sandals, but they look worn out and I have a covering on my body, but it looks like an old worn dress, and it looks plain like an off white or grey, maybe because it's dirty.

Merlin: Are you alone walking on this path?

Ericka: No. My brother is walking with me, and there is an ox in front of me, and there are a lot of people on this path, too!

Merlin: Who is your brother? May I call you Hannah?

Ericka: Yes, you may call me Hannah! I'm with my brother James!

Merlin: Hannah, where are you and your brother James going?

Ericka: We are going to listen to The Teacher teach!

Merlin: Who is the Teacher, Hannah?

Ericka: He is my eldest brother!

Merlin: Hannah what is the name of your eldest brother who is teaching?

Ericka: Jeshua is my eldest brother!

Merlin: Oh, Jeshua is your brother? What is Jeshua teaching?

Ericka: How to bless others and to be blessed!

Merlin: So, Hannah, let us go forward to a time in that lifetime when you spoke to your brother Jeshua. Where are you now?

Ericka: I am happy to see my brother Jeshua, and I run to him as I always do. My brother tells me that he must leave for a while, but he will return.

Merlin: Where is your brother going, Hannah?

Ericka: My brother is going to Jerusalem for Passover with my brothers and sisters.

Merlin: Will you be there, Hannah?

Ericka: Yes, with my mother and brothers!

Merlin: Did your brother Jeshua say anything else?

Ericka: Yes, he told me he is the Lamb and he will be sacrificed (crying).

Merlin: How does that make you feel, Hannah?

Ericka: Heartbroken!

Merlin: Now, let's move on later while you are in Jerusalem. Tell me, what happened there? What did you see and experience?

Ericka: I'm on the tree and I see many of our sisters on the tree. My brother Jeshua was there. My mother is below me with my brother James and Mary Magdalene. They are all crying! I'm scared, I'm in pain, I can't breathe! Help me! I can't breathe...

Merlin: Hannah, what happens next?

Ericka: I'm out of my body, the sky is black, and the Earth is rumbling as in an earthquake!

Merlin: Is there anyone with you while you are watching your death and the death of your brother?

Ericka: An Angel is with me and commands me to go into her!

Merlin: Who is the Angel talking about?

Ericka: My brother Jeshua's wife, Mary!

Merlin: Now, may I speak to Ericka?

Ericka: Yes.

Merlin: Ericka, you look confused, where are you now?

Ericka: I'm back in the film room and I can't believe what I just saw! So, I'm the daughter of Jeshua and Mary

Magdalene? How can this be, this is not what we were taught as Christians! Wait, I see someone coming in! Is it true?

Merlin: Who is with you now, Ericka?

Ericka: Jeshua and Mary Magdalene!

Merlin: Do they answer you?

Ericka: Yes, Jeshua says it's true that I was his daughter and Mary, his wife, is my mother!

Merlin: Do you believe this Ericka?

Ericka: I don't know what to think, but it explains my life and why I have certain gifts, but ... really? Come on! What a burden to have! Why am I here, and why did I choose to come here? I want to stay with Jeshua, I don't want to be here on this evil planet!

Merlin: Ericka, we're running out of time, so I'm going to bring you back to the present and you will remember all that we have talked about. After you leave you will think about what this all means to you and reflect on this lifetime, and God will show you why you are here in his own divine timing. I'm going to count backwards in 5, 4, 3, 2, 1, and open your eyes!

"As I woke up, I was amazed at what this regression discovered, but afterward I was confused and still filled with questions. At the time, I did not believe in it because it sounded 'out there.' To this day I find it a mystery but have learned about humility and unconditional love for all. We all have past lives whether we believe it or not. We are all souls learning and experiencing. No matter who we were or what we've done in the past, it shapes our future, and not only the world's future but our own story. I have personally gone through six to seven past life regressions. I've seen my behaviors and I even dream about past lives or memories. I have even met people that shared a past life with me. Even the author of this book was my mother in two or three occasions, and my sister and my aunt. I have been a queen twice, and I have been a princess three times that I recall, and I have been a commoner as well. I also learned that it doesn't matter who we were but what we've learned.

"In my life now, I have met my Twin Flame, who has shared past lives with me, but he found me. He is someone who I never thought he would be, and as I got to know him, I saw things in him that mirrored back to me. I'm learning about myself now and growing myself. When you experience this at first you are skeptical. But then I grew and had an open mind. There is more to God and the universe then meets the eye. It's up to everyone to seek their truth within themselves. Thank you for my telling this part of my life's story!"

Chapter 25 Hannah Remembers Jeshua and Mary Magdalene's Wedding Feast at Bethany, CE 30 7/21/2017

Hannah: "Jeshua is speaking at his wedding feast in Aramaic. He said, 'Be of great light and love!'" (Aramaic word)

Marcia: "Thank you. That's beautiful. Thank you."

Hannah: "I remember the supper. Mother Mary is telling me what to do. Mother Mary is teaching me how to set the table, to prepare the foods. She is teaching me how this is done, how that is done. Those were normal things that a Hebrew girl would be taught.

"Then, while serving the disciples, my brother, Jeshua, and his wife held my hand. He actually took it, looked at me and said something very intensely. They were toasting the occasion, too. Mary Magdalene blushee and, many glasses were raised to the happy couple."

Marcia: "Did Jeshua get married officially there, or was it earlier?"

Hannah: "I believe they had already been married, and this was just the celebration. It was festive. Mary wore a deep blue garment. She glowed with love for Jeshua. There were many sweets and lots of hummus and dipping into the common bowl. Someone had killed a lamb. The table was laid with everything, and more. I feel there were some windows in this place. You could hear the children playing outside and everything was very powerful, as it always was with Jeshua. Radiating love and joy, he was smiling. Mary was smiling. All were happy for the day.

"I remember lots of figs, lots of sweets and fresh vegetables. I remember the bread dipped into the butter, a kind of humus like today, also milk and yogurt. I feel that I would have been helping her to get dressed, and I think we were all wearing white. The sun is very bright. Mother Mary prepared for this. I see a lot of flowers around, and there may have been only the family, and some of the disciples

"Mary Magdalene has a bouquet of flowers. I think we were in Bethany as a lot of the disciples were there!"

Marcia: "Hannah, do you remember Mother Mary? Do you remember what she was like?"

Hannah: "She was like Jeshua. She pushed love above all. She was very joyful. I cannot explain anything else about her. She was beautiful and quiet.

"I remember Jeshua calling himself the bridegroom and she, Mary Magdalene, the bride. That was actually the marriage. All this was in secret as no one needed to know. Mother Mary did anticipate the tragedy. How she managed to carry on I don't know."

Marcia: "What did you mean by 'all in secret'?"

Hannah: "I don't know—I think it was Mother Mary's secret. She knew that Jeshua would be taken from us, from her. I think Mary Magdalene knew, too."

Marcia: "Can you describe Mother Mary's attitude towards life?"

Hannah: "She was very delicate... um. She was serene and she always pushed love above all. I can't explain anything else about her."

The Regression Continues

Hannah: "I remember serving. And his word to me, now that I think about that, it seems he had given me a message about his death and mine, in Aramaic. He meant to tell me never to lose hope. That was the reason why he took my arm and said those words. I was to lose him someday soon. What I didn't know was that there was more waiting for me. He tried to warn me, to encourage me."

Hannah Recollects the Crucifixion of Jeshua and Herself

Marcia: "Go ahead now, Hannah."

Hannah: "I was betrothed to be with Adam. But I never got to be with Adam because I (sobbing) died on the cross— my own cross!"

(Note: Hannah suddenly switched to another scene in her lifetime. She was one of Jeshua's followers and had apparently been snatched by the Romans, accused as one of them, taken and crucified. I cannot imagine the horror! The scene opens with Hannah on the cross the same day Jeshua is crucified).

Hannah: "I could see Jeshua, too, from the cross. They have taken him down from the cross. Oh, my! Lightning struck, it has grown dark. My brother Jeshua is gone. I saw him die, and very suddenly they took him down. I was growing colder and colder, and I couldn't breathe. My Mother Mary was holding her sides and crying with such great grief. She just wailed and wailed. She was beside herself. The others, Mary and the other Mary were in the distance. As I was on that cross crying out to God and the bystanders 'I don't know what I did to deserve to die,' I remember that the Angel told me that Mary Magdalene was pregnant. 'As you leave your body when you die, go into her'.

"And, I didn't even experience heaven. Instead, I just immediately went into Mary's body. I experienced myself. My death on the cross was terrible. I grew colder and colder and I didn't understand why anyone would do this to me, as I had not done anything wrong. Why had this happened to me, why was this happening to me, why was this just such an evil world? I couldn't understand."

Marcia: "It was such a horrible day for Mother Mary. A horrible day for you, for everyone we loved. Thank you, Hannah, for your memories. I am so sorry it had to happen to you. Let's move back instead to the joyful day of Mary Magdalene with Jeshua."

Author notes:

This account of Hannah is short. It does reflect the joy of the wedding day of Jeshua and Mary Magdalene. However, it is tinged with great sorrow knowing that Jeshua had to endure the cross and so did his beloved younger sister. She speaks in a tone that would indicate an age somewhere between 13 and 17. So, it's very honest, immature and genuinely young.

Reference:

Starbird, M. retrieved 2018, published 2005 Bear and Co. Publishing. *Mary Magdalene Bride in Exile.* Starbird claimed that any of Jesus' known followers were subject to certain death in Palestine and would have been sought out.

It is so unfortunate that little Hannah went through this, but she tells of her immediate reincarnation as Sarah, daughter of Mary Magdalene and Jeshua. Her name, Sarah, means princess in Egyptian. That story is presented in Chapter 25 narrated by Ericka Stout.

Chapter 26 Past Lifetime Regression of John the Beloved Disciple

Note: Marcia is acting as hypnotist, and Jim (another name given to the one who is being regressed).

Marcia: "You're at the doorway of that past life. I sense that we need to clear some anxiety. I think we are going to have a very interesting session, as this information is already in your consciousness and in your energy body. We're going to release all fear with whatever wants to come forward.

"We ask the higher self to guide you along with angels and guides to clear any anxiety. When you walk through the door you will be cleared of anxiety. When I count to three and snap you are going to feel the most awesome love of the Creator, and you are going to feel so good. None of this will be revealed to anyone should you wish to keep it confidential. We'll going to call on this all-encompassing love to come down upon you. 1, 2, 3. We call upon the white light of Christ Consciousness. Your guides and angels love you unconditionally. If it is their will, you will go to this lifetime. And if it is not their will, then you will go to another lifetime."

Marcia: "Are you feeling any lighter or better?"

Jim: "Yes."

Marcia: "Shall we increase the love light vibration, or proceed?"

Jim: "Proceed."

Marcia: "During your trips I will ask questions you may answer mentally but be sure to answer the questions and not ignore them. The fog still surrounds you. It will now disappear. The fog is gone. You are walking along. Do you have a sense of where you are?"

Jim: "I see a man that looks like he has a beard and the color of his clothing is changing. All I am seeing is a man wearing a turban."

Marcia: "Continue looking around you. Can you sense why this day is a happy day? Observe all the detail. Look down at your feet."

Jim: "My feet are in sandals. My garment is silky and white. I also see a total desert."

Marcia: "Is anyone with you?"

Jim: "I sense a man and other people. I do feel like I am leading people forward. I turn around and look and I am seeing a large man with a big head, bald on top. Heavier, younger men are around and he's on the right. Two other younger men on the side aren't as clear to me. I feel like there are more people somewhere, but I don't really sense them."

Marcia: "Do you happen to know the names of the men you are seeing; the bigger man's name?"

Jim: "Paul is the bigger man, the other Samuel, and the other Lukas."

Marcia: "Would you, by chance, have a name for yourself in this lifetime?"

Jim: "My immediate sense is John. That's what is coming through. Later I'm at a banquet at the head of the table, and once again I am not getting a full visual detail. Our table is indoors with a tent around it. Money or gold is on the table, people drinking from chalices, too. It was wonderful and a lot of it was humdrum.

"Now there is another scene in which I am near a tomb, but where is Jeshua? What has happened to him? He was laid here in this tomb but now it's empty and no one knows why. I am getting a sense that he is nearby, but I am not sure."

Marcia: "Let's go back to that idea. You say you feel Jeshua is nearby. Where is he, then, or is he in Spirit over-lighting you?"

Jim: "No, he is not in Spirit. He is nearby. We step outside the tomb. Jeshua is standing outside the tomb! We are weeping and hugging for joy, and Jeshua is speaking. He says, 'You see, I said to have faith that I would be back.' And we are astounded, looking at him. He is light filled. It is the physical Jeshua. He shows us himself."

Marcia: "This is all good information. Now I am going to move you to the next part of this lifetime. In a moment I am going to have you go to five years later. When I count one, two three, you will go to another scene in this life five years later. 1, 2, 3. Where are you?"

Jim as John: "I am holding scrolls. I am teaching in a grove today to a small group of people, maybe fifty to seventy people. I am teaching the gospel, spreading the gospel. I am carrying the books, and they are ancient texts that I have been entrusted with. We are in India. I have others with me, Mark and another Lukas. We're preaching the good news of the Way, as the Master had taught us. We are healing in his name, and we are making people happier, lighter in their burdens. That is all I can recall. I'm coming back to my present life. I am feeling full of this wonderful energy we brought with the love of Jeshua."

Chapter 27 The Grail Artifacts Speak at Bob Murray's Study in Heaven

Interview in heaven at Bob Murray's home

Channeled by Marcia McMahon

Marcia: "Good morning, Bob Murray! I've come to your door."

Bob: "Welcome to my writing room, and my fire and my dog. Make yourself comfortable in the chair or on the sofa."

Marcia: "Well, as you know I am in a conundrum about many things of late, and of course in my questions about Joseph of Arimathea. Are you free right now to speak to me, Bob?"

Bob: "Surround yourself completely in the light and come up to the higher vibrations of this room. Relax and adjust to the surroundings here. As you look around, what do you see?"

Marcia: "I'm seeing a special tree outside your window and it's blossoming. I feel that it is a graft from Joseph of Arimathea's Thorn Tree. I'm looking around at old leather-bound books, play scripts dating thousands of years back, biblical manuscripts, different accounts of Jeshua. I'm seeing all kinds of them, some in ancient urns and some of them are painted, and other urns are containing old scrolls.

"There are urns here that were found in the Egyptian desert regarding Mary Magdalene's story, and missing pieces of wood from Joseph's boat. All these artifacts are glowing with energy and love and seem to come alive. They are almost like the mysteries at the museum. These artifacts have a life of their own."

Bob: "Yes, you're getting it. I've assembled the collection of artifacts for you to look at."

Marcia: "I'm seeing a piece of the Holy Cross and a very rugged looking nail. I'm gazing at some thorns from Jeshua's crown. I'm looking at the chalice that was used at the Last Supper, which was a very simple one of stone or limestone."

Bob: "You're welcome to this. I've arranged to have these on loan from Joseph of Arimathea! You see, I've assembled an entire grail quest in my study for you right now. You can choose any one of these artifacts to open and they will speak to you."

Marcia: "What about your advice, Bob?"

Bob: "No, I think it is more fun this way, as you need to have a little fun."

Marcia: "And frankly, Bob, I'm still looking around. The wood from the boat is calling me first."

Bob: "Just go over and touch the wood that is sitting on my display table. Tell me what the wood has to say."

The Wood from Joseph's Ship

Marcia: "This is the wood from one of Joseph's many ships. The wood seems to say that it's very tired from making so many trips back and forth from England to Palestine, and back. Then it was eventually lost in a shipwreck sometime after 300 AD. This was the wooden ship in which all the disciples travelled from Palestine to Egypt. Then it still survived after the oars and sails were removed when the disciples were stranded at sea relying only on the wind.

"The ship came ashore on the island of Crete where it was repaired, and new oars and sails were added. During that time there were opportunities that Joseph provided for food and shelter, and of course he came along on another ship to make sure everything was going smoothly.

"The ship was once again ready to sail, and it had a special name. I'm getting the words 'maiden voyage,' but I'm not sure if that's the proper meaning. Well, it was certainly used for a lot of the maidens that needed to escape those who were not supportive of Jeshua around Palestine.

"We eventually landed on the shores of France. I'm being reminded where the little chapel is that was dedicated to Sarah and Mary Magdalene at Saint Marie de le Mar. Inside the grotto there are many other artifacts housed below the chapel, containing secrets that the Catholic Church has hidden.

"I'm looking at these artifacts that are here. Are there any others displayed today?"

Bob, "Yes if you look to the right you will see a Black Madonna. Go ahead and touch the Black Madonna or her belly for good luck."

The Black Madonna

Marcia: "I'm seeing Sarah. I see that the black Madonna resembles a darker girl who could be from Egypt. She was rumored to be the slave girl of Mary Magdalene, but that was only a decoy for Sarah, who was born in Egypt."

The Black Madonna speaks: "Thousands of pilgrims have touched me and regained their health, through believing in the power of healing from Mary Magdalene and Jeshua. I am the most sacred of relics. I come to speak to you of the story of Sarah today."

Sarah: "In this region of France there were many who knew of my real identity. The priest, whom you know, dug up these finds. He was well aware that there was an only child, and it was myself. He was paid a ransom note from the Catholic Church for recovering this material. He actually found my bones, that shovel, and other precious relics including part of the true cross and other fragments of the gospels of Mary Magdalene that were located there.

"What was revealed was so upsetting to the Church hierarchy that they decided to make this priest very wealthy and let him live out his days in luxury. Then the Church confiscated the relics, the gospels, and other items of Mary Magdalene. They're now sealed somewhere deep inside the Vatican library and available only to the trusted few."

Marcia: "This is as interesting as *The DaVinci Code*, so please do go on, Sarah."

Sarah: "You know me or my soul aspect as Ericka, but she does not contain the full record of the accounting of what really happened in my life, so I will continue telling the story.

"When we arrived, I was a toddler and my mother and I stayed with you, Martha, in a cave for a while. You were my aunt and you took good care of me. Mother was very busy with her new way of mastery. There were many followers back then, but it was all held in secret within the cave.

Mother and I stayed in this region of Southern France, in Languedoc, from three to ten years.

"We heard of the Druids welcoming us because Uncle Joseph had been associated with the area of Cornwall known as the Summerland. That area is where Uncle Joseph and Jeshua had landed at one time. My father, Jeshua, came to visit me both in dreams and in the flesh. He was always very light-hearted and made me laugh.

"My mother, Mary, is a little bit more serious and she does a lot of meditation. But you liked to take me out and teach me the ways of nature in the woods, by the streams and wells.

"Next, we went to England to visit the Summerland and the tin mines of Wales. Uncle Joseph was ready for us to board ship. He came to get us all, with the disciple Philip and some others. The name of another, Zacheus, came with us, too, and he was a little bit difficult.

"I was often seasick. We had provisions with us. Joseph was manning the ship. He sailed all around Great Britain. A number of other followers came later. Joseph actually visited three sacred sites. On the tip of Cornwall, you will notice that we landed on an island, later called Michael's Mount. Joseph hired a caravan and some wagons, and we got to know the local people called Druids. They took us up the Magdalene Way, an ancient druid path, to what you know today as Glastonbury.

"There my mother initiated the Druids into the Holy Divine Feminine, and she also shared me by passing me around from person to person around an outside fire. I think you will remember this well, Martha."

Marcia: "Yes, I do recall some of this. Can you tell me with any accuracy, Sarah, how long we were in Glastonbury and when did we return to France?"

Sarah: "I'm feeling that my father Jeshua did visit in Glastonbury and was with my mother. For three days she went into the silence where she would be able to see and converse with him. During that time, I was able to see him as well. We had a feast there as the Druids knew that Jeshua had come. We walked all around looking for a safe land where we could stay.

"Since our uncle Joseph was very wealthy, it wasn't hard to find people who were willing to help. I remember that Uncle Joseph planted some thorns from Jeshua's crown of thorns, and it was said that they would bloom each year. We had several small huts there, and I remember that I was always cold. I had come up from Egypt, but this place was cold. You didn't like it either, Martha.

"We eventually settled in the land of Glastonbury and Avalon. Some of the disciples, the Essenes as we know them, settled with us. Great Grandmother Anna loved it there as she was related to Uncle Joseph and she was a very wonderful lady. Grandmother Mary Anna, the mother of Jeshua, also stayed with us for a long time.

"At some point my mother, Mary Magdalene, and I decided to migrate back to the region of Languedoc. We went because we liked the weather and Mary felt that she could do her writing in the cave more easily. She also felt that she had a mission to educate people in France and that France would one day become the home of her people. There were Jews in France who welcomed us. And, of course, we had a small community in Languedoc, as Joseph's lands were scattered throughout the area.

"Martha decided to stay in Glastonbury and study with the Druids. She was always studying, and she loved books and writings. She had little ones in her care as she grew older there, and Mother Mary came frequently to visit, as did Jeshua. But, the community in Glastonbury was a mixture of traditions including both Druid and the New Way. Frequently we would voyage from our home in Languedoc to Glastonbury and back and forth.

"You are holding a piece of the original ship and that was the biggest and oldest ship that uncle Joseph sailed. He was a master of many things: business, sailing, and interpersonal relations. He also could keep track of numbers very well. He actually was an uncle to us, a great-uncle.

"I had a lot to say for a little Black Madonna statue, but I am speaking from the Akashic records, and I am the one known as Sarah, from Egypt and France. I loved my mother and was devoted to her as she was to me, and we completed our mission in France. There are manuscripts remaining somewhere in a cave where my mother lived."

Marcia: "I know I would like to ask to connect with the relic of the True Cross if there is such a thing. And while I'm at Father Murray's house, I can see there about fifteen different pieces of it, all looking like rather different timbers: one of olive wood, one of dogwood and one of the thorn tree".

Bob: "Just pick your choice of wood you wish to speak to."

Marcia McMahon

The Olive Tree

"Now I'm picking up one of the pieces of wood from the cross. It looks to me to be very much like an olive wood tree, possibly from The Garden of Gethsemane. The tree is crying out for help as an axe was applied to it. The tree is screaming in agony. It does not want to be chopped down. It rebels against the thought of having this Son of God hanging on this tree. The olive tree only wants to be left alone, to live and to grow—just like Jeshua should be left alone to grow his following and continue his teachings.

"The Romans are taking an axe to me. I'm a very old tree that has given much shade and comfort to those who have rested here in the Garden of Gethsemane. Today is a particularly difficult day, a day that I wish to forget as I am being chopped down for the purpose of a crucifixion.

"Any crucifixion is horrible. I don't want to wear that beautiful man on my branches. I feel ashamed and confused, for on me was shed the blood of innocents. All through the streets I was dragged, like some kind of criminal, and I bore this human body in between my branches. I felt the emotions of Jeshua as he was dying there on the cross, made from me. I rebelled against the creator and I asked how he could create me to kill an innocent human, especially as I wanted to be a blessing to Jeshua. Nails were driven into my flesh, too, as a horrific thing also happened to me on that day.

"Bloodstained and in agony, Jeshua cried out in a loud voice and said, 'It is over.' We both assumed a new form when that happened, for I was with him as he journeyed through the many mansions and remained unseen in Hades, until that new day. Joseph of Arimathea came with Nicodemus to take the body down, and then saved pieces of

163

myself for later generations to admire! I felt only shame. I wanted not to be the artefact.

"I tell you there is nothing to admire in being the instrument of such torture and execution. Yes, there are still fragments of me both on the Earth plane and, also, in the heavenly plane. It's forever part of the Akashic records of what the Romans did to a great teacher and Son of God. I do not want your reverence, but I will give you comfort. If you touch me, there are still remnants there of the blood of the teacher, Jeshua.

"This was never meant to be, and I am still ashamed of my branches, which were only meant to give life and shade in return. I am the olive tree and I send out peace to all those who look upon me. I am finished."

Marcia: "Father Bob, I'm looking around at the other artifacts, but I'm growing a little bit weary. May I come and visit again?"

Bob: "I suggest a brief break and come back in about an hour. I think you'll find another artifact that is willing to speak with you and that you will like. The olive tree was particularly difficult, but there are others waiting for you and I'm available anytime."

Sometime later:

Marcia: "Hello again, Bob, I'm back."

Bob: "Go ahead, just take your time, and look around."

The Chalice Speaks

Marcia: "I think I've come to the chalice, the holy grail of holy grails."

Bob: "Keep going, just describe it."

Marcia: "It is white carved limestone with an insignia on it. The insignia seems to stand for Jesus Christ or a family crest. But it's not an insignia that I recognize in this language. Perhaps it is in Aramaic.

"I'm tuning in to the object, which is a cup that held the wine. It also held tears and then Joseph removed it (after the supper) and used it to hold the blood as his nephew was dying.

"Joseph revered Jeshua for his light and his amazing work. Because Joseph held the chalice that Jeshua used as the ordained Messiah, he did everything possible to preserve the cup of the Last Supper. When Jeshua called it his blood and body, then it later became the relic. This happened recently after the crucifixion. Joseph did not intend to create a cult of the relic. He merely intended to honor its memory as Jeshua asked all of his followers to do."

Sometime later I return to Bob's house in Sussex on the other side.

Marcia: "Are you busy, Bob? I see that I'm back with you again."

Bob, "Yes, welcome again to my humble abode which is serving as the living museum of the relics of the Holy Grail. This time Joseph is also here with me, and he will have a message for you later. So, just take your time and ease into the surroundings. Look about as you were in the midst of describing the rays of light from the grail, the holy chalice. So, tune in and see what the chalice wants to say, as well."

Marcia: "The original chalice was a white, carved limestone drinking cup that was a little deeper than most. It had an insignia of the family name on it. It was the common cup used at the Last Supper.

165

"Jeshua had instructed the disciples to do this in remembrance of him. The cup carried Jeshua's vibrations and the cup was also inscribed with his saying that would be symbolic of his blood. Later, Joseph took the same cup when he went to take down the body of Jeshua. It was a very sad day.

"Since the cup was used for the Last Supper, it was also used to collect the blood of the dead Christ. It was to be a holy relic, much like the head of John the Baptist. Healings were said to spring from this cup. Miracles, numerous healings of relationships, as well as limbs were restored. That was the power of the blood, and the cup. After Joseph brought it by ship to Britain, I feel that it's the same cup as other cups that were being used for communion at that time. Later the use of metal cups began in Britain, as the common cup of communion had been adopted then."

The Crown of Thorns and the Thorn Tree at Glastonbury

"Joseph also brought the crown of thorns and planted a thorn from which a thorn tree grew. To this day, the thorn tree is in Glastonbury and still blooming. While visiting Glastonbury, our guide told us that the thorn tree produces blossoms on both Christmas and on Easter. These blossoms are placed on the Queen's table the morning on both of these holidays. The thorn tree is not a fiction. The monks that lived at Glastonbury Abbey may have pruned it back in the Middle Ages, but basically it is of the same genus and species as the original thorn tree that Joseph planted."

More on the Holy Chalice or Grail Cup

"While Joseph was giving drinks from the holy cup and distributing the healing waters to those who drank it, the cup accidentally fell into a well. The well waters lay deep in the Earth and were sacred. Joseph wanted everyone to get a drink from the well, as the cup ended up at the bottom.

"The waters were considered sacred, and some came to believe later that the iron that flows from the Glastonbury well is actually symbolic of the blood of Christ, while the white well is symbolic of Mary Magdalene or Mother Mary. There are two main wells, but also many others too numerous to name. It is impossible to see now-at which well the accident happened, but the cup fell in very deeply.

"And so, from this spring the entire Grail legend sprang forth—from the well. Many pilgrims were on a Grail search for centuries trying to find Joseph's holy cup, which was considered the ultimate Grail prize. The Grail of course was considered as the source for the miraculous healing of the waters there. Little was known about the true meaning of the Grail. Knights died for it and sought it in the Holy Land, but it remained in England or 'Angle land' for centuries.

"To this day, the well is still sacred and, if you go to Glastonbury Abbey, you will see one small well that is covered with glass. That is most likely the well. And so, it is impossible to say now where the Grail cup ended up. It is not important, but the vibrations of Christ sharing his blood with all his disciples are an important DNA activation for all.

"Jeshua knew that all cannot be partaking in the ceremony and that all would not be disciples. He knew that all would not be part of the holy bloodline. So, he devised this plan when it came his time, to recognize that he would have to leave the Earth plane. Even that terrible day was not necessarily in the Divine Plan, but it ended up that way. And so, thousands of miracles have happened with this Holy Grail cup, and there is still a cup there in Glastonbury, England today. It is not the original cup by any means! It is a different cup used in sacred ceremonies called the 'blue chalice'.

"But it is sanctifying to the holder, and it contains the same energies of Jeshua's sacred blood. We encourage all pilgrims to bear this in mind, to remember that the real Grail is the divine feminine of Mary Magdalene. Her contribution of the child to the bloodline is far more significant. The giving and sharing of the meal at the Last Supper was equally significant for the Abbey and signified a new way of life for the believer."

Veronica's Veil and the Shroud of Turin

At the end of my life as Martha, I believe I came into possession of Jeshua's small face cloth known as the Veronica Veil. I know some people think it is a forgery, but I differ. There were Jeshua's signature marks including roman coins in the eyes dating from that timeline, as well as the pollen in the fabric from the area of the same location. Also, the face seems to be magically much like Jeshua's. I suppose I asked him, and he confirmed it was true. I will look for that message. He said these images were necessary for the doubting Thomas's out there. Unfortunately, it has had the opposite effect, and the doubters attack all-the more.

Yes, the Shroud of Turin has yet to be authenticated completely by other means. It was studied by scientists in a

Vatican-science collaboration. The bloodstains are real human blood. Carbon 14 dating is not as accurate as it should be, as it dates to a later period than first century. I believe the Shroud of Turin is genuine. It has the Roman coins on Jeshua's eyes. There are no brush marks on the cloth, and it was not painted. It is almost as if it was an X ray of Jeshua's resurrection, emanating a mysterious light. The figure bears crucifixion marks on his hands, wrists and feet. It is hard to imagine forgers doing this kind of work. It is regarded as genuine by the Vatican.

Mary Magdalene's Alabaster Jar

Mary of Bethany: "My dear Marcia, this is your sister Mary of Bethany. I am pleased to come forth this day after joining the Church. Jeshua was reminding you of our time together in Bethany.

"You have been asked to create many things. A great deal of wisdom has poured forth from you like I used to do. You used to marvel at me, but you were the more outgoing of the two of us. You were friendly and well-versed and worldly-wise. I was the quiet one that sat at the feet of the Master. I was the lady with the alabaster jar and, yes, it was a very difficult task and one I did with great love and affection for the Master Jeshua.

"The alabaster jar contained spikenard and occupied a special place. It was kept in the house for a very long time and kept for Jeshua alone. He had told me that he would soon be made to suffer and die. It broke my heart, as I know it broke yours. We were very much a family—you, Jeshua and I, together with our brother Lazarus and all of the disciples.

169

"We spent the last two years traveling and learning his healing methods. We would bring great light into our lungs and meditate upon the sun whatever our day. We would turn our gaze and inhale and call upon the sun's rays for healing. Here's what I recommend that you do for your healing now, my dear sister Martha. You will achieve your healing; have no doubt, whatever symptoms and side effects you have from the treatments. Try the best you can to overlook them, and do use your medicinal herbs, by all means. And when necessary, take the drugs, but do try to wean off the pharmaceutical medicines. The herbs are much gentler and agree with you so much more."

Holy Wednesday

Mary continues: "As I was saying, on that fateful day of Wednesday Jeshua had come to the house. We had just finished washing his feet. And then it occurred to me to go and get the alabaster jar. I was so devastated that I washed his feet with my tears and wiped it with my reddish hair. When you drew me and painted me, you drew me quite correctly as you remember. I would suggest bringing these to the next retreat and talking most particularly about the picture you drew there and the painting you made of Jeshua by the Sea of Galilee, during his resurrection time! That was a painting! And they should be made available for sale. So many will want to know your personal experience with Jeshua. I am slowly revealing these titbits to your mind so that you can remember once again."

Marcia: "Mary, my darling sister, can you explain where our brother was in the lower compartment of the tomb? Or was he buried all the way down four stories and a separate side of the house?"

Mary: "He was buried where you thought, right on the lower level of the home and the current home also leads down the stairs to the secret chamber. I am very delighted that you got to see our old home, for it was very spectacular in its day, and it was a fitting place for the conception of our beloved child, Sarah. You knew or suspected that I was pregnant, but you didn't ask until sometime later. Mother Mary knew by instinct that I had been impregnated."

Marcia: "May I ask, Mary dear, how this came to be, whether by natural means or as a light conceived child?"

Mary: "By the time I had completed the rituals that were held inside the tomb of the pharaohs in my initiations in the Temple of Isis, for many years, I thought that Isis had put a spell on me herself and that she was responsible for my being barren. I only learned later that night that barrenness was due to my guilt over having had my heart broken and going to Bethany, and beyond to Magdala where our mother was from. And so, my early years of broken-heartedness and sexuality brought me infertility. It seemed to be related to some sort of disease that I had which later Jeshua healed me of. And then I think I was able to conceive the child in a natural way. It was not assisted by heaven. Jeshua was a man and it was not as if I was not a woman. These Church dogmas that say that I conceived my little one with only the power of God is not so, my friend.

"We had normal marital relations in our home in Bethany. No one was to know that we were secretly married for fear of the Romans. Jeshua told me many times that he would suffer and die. My heart could not bear it, and yet the thought of his seed within me gave me reason for hope. I would carry on a new generation that would be his offspring. As you know, Jeshua had another wife and family in Jerusalem with Miriam of Tyana. We three got along, but during those last days Jeshua gave all his attention to me, and of course to you, my dear sister Martha. He felt it necessary that the other family be held in secrecy, and he was very careful never to offend Miriam or me with any of the knowledge that was going on in either of our lives. So, he chose me for his last years and I felt so privileged!

"I had felt so deprived when he took Miriam to India to learn the ways of the hidden teachings of the Masters. As you know, there are records that reported Jeshua attending school. So yes, it was a natural conception, and you are in touch with that part of the soul known as Erica, who is my beloved child from long, long ago. I still watch over you both with great care, as I understand that you have gone through so much.

"You and I used to prepare a grain and vegetable diet for the very sick, and they were able to consume it and recover in some cases. You will remember these things, Martha, and I tell you that you will heal many people with your diet knowledge now. I am so glad that we were able to give you these uplifting energies at the church, the story today of our lives and times in Bethany. I am pleased that you cherish my memory, for I am Mary of Bethany, also known as Mary Magdalene. And I am delighted with your progress on the Earth plane toward world peace and toward the attainment of such worthy goals.

"I would like to now offer a silent blessing to each one of these people at the retreat today, and I would like to ask that there be unity and support of my channel, my dear beloved sister, and also support amongst you for the greater healing of mankind. Both Jeshua and I would like to observe a few minutes of silence so I can work on your energy fields and give you an energetic healing and an encoded message for healing personal and global issues. I am now visualizing a rose that is unfolding. Through this holy upgrade of energetic codes from cosmic forces in the universe, we are going to anoint you with rose oil and rose water.

"While there are other subtle aspects of myself present in your groups, I ascended with Jeshua at that time. There are still needed soul aspects of me in the world, and there has been an appearance of the master Jeshua in America. I tell you this is truth. Jeshua will not come on the clouds to save you, but you must find a way to attain inner mastery and thereby move to the 5th dimension yourselves."

Chapter 28 Joseph of Arimathea Speaks on the Meaning of the Grail

Marcia, "Good evening, Bob. Is Joseph of Arimathea here to speak with me concerning his story of long ago?"

Bob: "Good evening, Marcia. I would suggest that you relax more into the vibe of Joseph and his many travels, his tin mines, in his great wealth and the ships that brought you safely from Palestine through France to England, and also around the Mediterranean area."

Marcia: "I am receiving an image of Joseph who is a very fatherly old gentleman, with long white hair and a beard. He is dressed in a rather simple long robe with a belt. I've seen that in the colder weather he would wear various coloured coats that were gifts from people that he knew around the world. He is speaking to me now."

Joseph: "As Joseph, I was well educated. I would compute mathematical calculations for the sea quickly in my mind. I could calculate equations for the size of the shipbuilding and, also, the tin mining, into the miniscule and back. As Joseph, I was a brilliant man with a great many skills and was also devoted to God. I devoted my mission to Jeshua Ben Joseph, as you know him, and I fought to save Jeshua's life. I was unsuccessful and, therefore, had the courage to go to a very violent Roman ruler, Pontius Pilate, and ask for the body of Jeshua. My funds helped to pave the way for his message throughout the Mediterranean world.

"I also owned many homes in many lands, among them of course the home in Bethany. There was another home in Jerusalem and there were homes in England, around Wales

174

and then further south in Mara Zion. There was a home in France, as well. All of these places were resting stops along the way for the disciples and for what became the various movements of The Way.

"I, Joseph, was the father figure and the protectorate of the mission of the one you know as Jeshua. I had agreed to this before my incarnation and I had done all I could in Jeshua's lifetime to protect him and the entire Clan of Essenes.

"My tin mines in Wales and Cornwall directly provided a good deal of wealth for all of these things and allowed many to travel freely throughout the Mediterranean and into the greater Sea.

"I was also the captain of a ship, a carpenter and builder of ships, and I was also the uncle of Jeshua. I was grandmother Anna's younger brother. I oversaw Mother Mary Anna's safety and became a father figure for her family for a number of years, after the passing of her husband, Joseph. I wasn't a man of words so much as a man of action, right action, and that meant everything to me! I had the wealth of the world at my disposal, but it was only destined for the sake of the mission. Wealth was never something I needed, even at the home in Bethany, which I administered from a distance with Martha, Mary, and Lazarus, and originally my wife.

"Eventually the home in Bethany became the mission home for Jeshua, as well. Both Lazarus and Mary Magdalene, my daughter, were adopted; therefore, I was more like an uncle. I was very seldom there except in the formative years and or short time. You, as Martha, knew me as Uncle Joseph, and you sensed my distance, but I tell you that I was always aware. I had seers with me that would assist me when there was a call that went out for help.

"There was the secret network of runners and interpreters and gifted psychics. Father Bob was one of these psychics that I travelled with at that time. He was as gifted then as he is now, and he kept me in good company. Also, of course, the lovely Princess Diana was there, as Grandmother Anna, with Mother Mary of course, and then you, Martha, my child. I told you, my child, the situation involved a complicated marriage and I'll leave it at that. I provided a lovely home where we could witness to the ministry of compassion and grace in the midst of such a harsh environment, while offering Jeshua a home as well.

"Being the protectorate, I was charged with helping Jeshua and even from taking him down from the cross and providing a burial chamber fitting for a Son of God such as he was. I also provided for the rest of the family as they needed to escape quickly from the Roman rule. There are many secrets that are yet-to-be-revealed concerning the true Grail and the birth of the real Church.

"Mother Mary was also charged with the protectorate of her children and her grandchildren, as well as protecting Martha and Mary Magdalene. We made many trips across the ocean, experienced some very devastating shipwrecks, but all with me as the master and captain. With my shipbuilders and me, a good sense of navigation by the stars, and the assistance of the seers, we were able to make it through to safety and return to God with our mission fulfilled.

"You are in touch with a soul aspect of me, and you should send this on. You are aware of the various things that went on in the three days Jeshua was buried in the tomb. That remains a very controversial subject and there are many reports. I urge you to use your own discretion as to what you remember from that lifetime and, also, what is told you by your sources. Each one must discern truth within the heart of the soul. I promise you that more will be revealed, and I am very glad to be once again in touch with you through Robert Murray.

"These surprises will seem never ending and your book will flower once it is published. We bless you in the light of the great Creator, and we are happy to contribute more at a later time. I am Joseph of Arimathea, the traveller, the shipbuilder, sea captain and protectorate."

Chapter 29 Grandmother Anna's Story. Princess Diana Reveals her Past Life as Anna, Grandmother of Jeshua

Marcia: "Good afternoon, Princess Diana. It's been so long since talking to you. Is now a good time?"

Princess Diana: "Certainly, Marcia. I'm ever so pleased that you asked me today to do the session regarding the Divine Feminine. In my lifetime I did represent the Divine Feminine in my fashion statement, and then later in many humanitarian works. I have been tirelessly working with my scribe Marcia for over fifteen years now on issues of world peace and what can be done to prevent terrorism, in particularly the Western Nations: my beloved Britain, England, and of course the United States. We see that Marcia's work has been fruitful though she has suffered a great deal as a result of putting the work ahead of her health on occasion.

"Yes, I was part of the Divine Feminine some two thousand years ago in your time. I was the mother of the Virgin Mary and known as Anna in that lifetime. Many of the Essenes who are my extended family also knew me as Grandmother Anna. It was my job to be the mother of that princess, to nurture her and to care for her so that she would be the one to carry the holy seed, as was long prophesied.

Anna: "I had originally come from that part of Britain that you now know as Wales. So, that pattern was in my genetic structure from a previous lifetime. You'll notice the same consonant in my name as Anna. I was beautiful then, I had reddish blond hair. But my beauty was not important as much as my function, the protector of all the Essene children, both my beloved daughter Marianna, and then of course my amazing grandson named Jeshua or Emmanuel.

"Mother Mary, as a young child, was offered to the temple at a very early age to study the mystery at Mount Carmel. I was devastated to have to give that little princess up! And that truly broke my heart for, by then, I was with my husband Joachim. We had a lovely, harmonious home in Nazareth, and we were well off. It was very hard to see my daughter, a mere six years old, go so far away. My husband Joachim had to take her by camel all the way to the monastery at Mount Carmel.

"At Mount Carmel there were austerities for my beloved daughter. She had to learn to control her temper or appetite and take care of herself at a very young age. I don't know everything about what happened to Marianna during that time except that she was initiated into very secret and privileged rights concerning the Divine Feminine, of which I wasn't aware, of course.

"There was a coming-out party for Mary and for all the young ladies, and at age thirteen a ceremony was held which I attended with Joachim. We were there among many Essenes. In attendance was a head Priestess, a representative of Isis, and for the Hebrew people a rabbi was also present. These two represented the masculine and feminine and were there to choose a woman who would bear the Messiah. There was a hush in the audience, which included a small number of parents attending a secret private service. It occurred up on Mount Carmel, where the beautiful vista of the world could be seen with the great sea behind it.

"A reading from the Torah scripture of the prophecy, noting the coming of the Messiah (Isaiah) was read with all due reverence. The dance that followed was like belly dancing as the girls were initiated into the Circle of the Rose. Each carried a red rose and wore swaying, beautiful gowns. As every girl had a perfect figure, all looked as though they could be the mother of the Messiah.

"But I knew something in my heart because an angel had come to me during Mary's preparation time. I was told that it would be Mariana who would bear the Messiah. And, after the sacred ceremony of the dance of the young maidens, a silence overcame the entire arena. The rose would be given to the maiden by the Headmistress and Headmaster of the school. There were votes cast as well from the audience, but the school made the final choice. When all the girls lined up it was little Marianna, who was only thirteen, who was chosen to be Mother of the Most-High anointed one, the Messiah. A hush overcame the audience. I wept as she had one tear roll down her beautiful cheeks. Since she had lived at Mount Carmel for most of her days, she was entirely lacking in practical household knowledge.

"Upon returning home to Nazareth, Mary engaged in normal things that children do as young teenagers. She gathered water at the well in the mornings, she learned to make bread, and I was teaching her all the household duties needed to be a good wife and mother to the Messiah.

"We kept the secret in our hearts and none of the members of our household, including our staff, knew about it.

"But it lay heavily on my heart because I understood that Mary would have suffering with this new assignment. I knew that a Messiah would not be an easy child to raise. This child still needed to be taught properly about languages and educated. Mary knew all her languages and learned to read and write at Mount Carmel, so now we had only a short, precious time, a year when I could prepare her.

"Mary learned bread making, languages and writing. She studied motherhood, how to raise a child, and which recipes are used for baking bread. Her education also included how to work with the male Kundalini energy, and how to please a man. This was all said in deepest secrecy and privacy between us, and we were very close.

"In those days, Joachim was a prosperous man, related to Joseph, my youngest brother. I'm speaking here of Uncle Joseph of Arimathea. Joseph of Arimathea also provided work for Joachim, who became involved with carpentry and shipbuilding in his employment.

"Joachim was a fine gentleman to have been married to. Joseph of Arimathea brought me on a ship all the way over to Wales since my mother was born there. My father was from Israel, so I carried both the bloodlines. I was raised in accordance with the Hebrew tradition of the day, and I briefly studied in the temple of Isis in Egypt as all properly educated girls did, as well. I was what you would call an Isis initiate, and was trained in raising the Kundalini and in many of the secret initiations that we studied then.

"My mother did tell me that I had an unusual birth. For some reason, she became pregnant late in life, which was totally unexpected. My parents were well off and, so, I was very protected and kept in the home most of the time. On my wedding day I was thrilled to be able to marry Joachim. He came from a good family line of the House of David, as we both did, so we knew that we were meant to be together.

"We had an inkling of this holy child on our wedding night. Angelic magic was happening and, before I even slept with Joachim, I knew that I had conceived. I had told Joachim about this and on our wedding night we agreed that we could feel an angelic presence with us, therefore we didn't officially begin our sexual relationship until Mary Anna had been born. So, you see that she and I were both born immaculate.

"The day when Mary went away, she was at the well and then she disappeared for a time. She was missing for the entire day and we became alarmed. Joachim had been busy all day at the shop and I had been occupied, when I noticed that she had been gone for too long. We sent other members of the family out to look for Mary. It was almost nightfall before we found her, and she was quite shaken up and had been crying. I didn't know exactly what had happened and, naturally, as a mother I feared the worst. I thought perhaps she had been raped, but I couldn't imagine that horror being allowed to happen to our darling daughter. Mary looked undefiled, joyful and confused through her tears. She came home safely and in the ensuing time between then and the following month I became aware that Mary was pregnant.

"She felt comfortable confiding in me what happened when she was away. First, she was too tired, but the next day and the following day we talked privately while we were weaving. Mary told me that the Archangel Gabriel came to her and said, 'I have a gift for you. You have been chosen among all the maidens to bear the Messiah,' and then he showed his full radiance to me. The Angel Gabriel is so gloriously white, and his light came into my body. Then I felt a pulsation—a joyful feeling while being there in my

182

room. I don't know how to describe it other than to tell you these things about it.'

"I (Anna) said, 'I don't know what to make of this. Do you think it is really the Archangel Gabriel who came to you when it would have been easier have a normal relationship and relations with a man? Are you, Marianna, certain that you're pregnant?' Marianna replied, 'Mother, I know as I feel it in my womb. I haven't had my moon cycle for six weeks. I've had no relations with any man and, therefore, I believe this happened when I met the Archangel Gabriel.'

"(Mother Anna) I said, 'That's fine, so now I want you to say this prayer,' and I gave her a special prayer that she could use for protection. If the village found out that she was pregnant, they would assume the worst and probably stone her to death. I was so heavy in my heart. It was a beautiful message about the angels, and Mary had never told a lie. Yet, I didn't know if it was really Divine, as I felt in my heart it may have been a case of rape. In either case, she was in eminent danger and I had to think for a long time before I could act on my best intentions for Marianna.

"I waited to tell anyone because I certainly wasn't sure what had happened, if it was the hand of the Divine. I didn't know that it would work out this way. I fully expected that Mary would become pregnant after marriage, not before. She had been dating a beautiful, older man named Joseph, and we had watched them interact and play together as children. Later he came to court her at the household on several occasions.

"Finally, Joseph proposed marriage to my daughter Mariana. And I breathed a sigh of relief as I thought that all would work out, as it should be. I never said much to my husband, Joachim, because I didn't believe that he would come around to the story. I doubted they would really believe that Mary had not committed adultery or trust the business about the angel. Joachim was a practical man and a good man, and he believed that she was the ordained carrier of the Messiah but not in this way. So, I kept it in within my heart to see fit to protect Mary as much as possible. I know Mary had thoughts of running away and going to another village to stay with my sister but decided not to do that.

"One fine day when Joseph came to call, he brought Mary a token of appreciation, some flowers. Later he asked for her hand in marriage from the both of us, as we sat around the table enjoying an evening meal. Mary was all smiles, and so were all of the family as well as myself and the other children, the brothers and sisters of Mary. We were all rejoicing and drinking wine and toasting the new couple. Joseph and Mary looked like the perfect couple, yet Mary knew that she was about nine weeks pregnant. Her condition was just beginning to show, and I was hoping that Joseph would not notice. Unfortunately, some time later Joseph did discover this. He was about to dissolve the relationship. He came to our home one evening for dinner when he and Mary were in the courtyard. They had a disagreement, and I could hear him calling her names she did not deserve.

"I knew in my heart that Mary was telling him the truth, although I had really no way to prove that. I remembered all about her special birth, and I remembered also about the angel who came to me on my marriage bed, so I knew Mary was a special child and I was out to protect her. Yes, without my protection, she certainly would have been stoned to death that evening.

"Mary came to me in confidence the next day weeping, saying that Joseph had broken off their engagement. She didn't know what to do except to go to another village, to her aunt's house to stay. For a long time, I prayed over this and I didn't know quite what to do. We had a way of contacting the angels and we had a method for prayers. Usually they were recitations and nothing more. At this particular time, I opened my heart to the angels and asked God to aid me sincerely, to help young Marianna.

"Later that week, Joseph returned to the house. He gave Mary a wedding gift and brought her clothing, as was the tradition of the time. At that point a wedding gown was in the making for Mary and all the guests were beginning to be invited. The invitations had been sent out. Joseph in his heart reconciled that Mary was meant to be his wife and he was meant to be her savior and protector.

"They held a joyful and bright wedding together in front of the entire village, and the rest of our extended families came from a long way to see Joseph and Mary united. Mary was a beautiful bride and Joseph became her older and handsome husband. There was feasting for three days until the marriage was to be consummated.

"But that too is another story. Mary told me that later it was never consummated. My heart sighed with a big sigh of relief knowing how pregnant she was, but she didn't show it with her gowns. They looked happy together, and that was what made my day. My heart sighed with relief."

*****

Mary: "In my womb I embodied the Son of God, Jeshua. I was almost at full term when Joseph and I had to make a journey to be taxed at Bethlehem. I was very pregnant and

185

almost ready to give birth, and the journey was difficult with many rocks along the way. We always had to be so careful of the Romans finding out who we were, for there had been rumors and talk of the Messiah being born and, of course, there were the stars in the sky that seemed to follow us everywhere we went.

"We stopped at Joseph's brother's inn and there was no room to be found. So, in haste we made a bed for myself to give birth and room for the others that were in our caravan, including my mother, Anna, the accompanying midwives and the servants that we had. I gave birth to my first-born and, finally, held my precious miracle. I named him Jeshua, and he was also called Emmanuel, from the scriptures of course.

"Grandmother Anna and the other midwife did a remarkable job for me, as there were unusual features about the birth of this child. First of all, he was born encased in a sack. Usually the sack is expelled differently. Some people in the East would have called this a miracle child, and truly he was my miracle child, my oldest of my clan.

"There were other brothers and sisters who came along later. I had many children. It is a myth that I was a virgin for all time and only bore Jeshua. There were many other children, and I was fully engaged in relations with my husband Joseph. And, yet, my first calling and my first duty were to raise the Messiah in a way that was appropriate.

"Joseph also considered the strangeness of the birth when the three wise men did arrive a few weeks later. They brought gold, frankincense, myrrh and other small gifts. There was the star at night thought to be a comet, so others who came to visit him were from the East. Balthazar was one such person, the grandfather of Mary Magdalene. The men with him were astrologers, and as such they possessed greater understanding of the stars and the timing of the coming of the Messiah.

"They were also gifted in their understanding and vision of who the special child was. They had gone to ask the Roman ruler of the day, Herod, about the whereabouts of the child. Joseph was given a dream by the Archangel Gabriel, who showed him briefly and bluntly what Herod would do regarding the murders of the children that were in Bethlehem.

"Almost as soon as I had given birth, I felt unspeakable joy and pride and everyone around me was so kind, even though it was a very humble affair.

"Then came the difficulty of leaving again quickly by caravan, all the way into Egypt, to protect the holy child. We journeyed along the coast for a while until Joseph of Arimathea had heard of our dilemma, and we were taken by ship straight away to Alexandria. There we had to live under an assumed name in order to protect us from the news getting back somehow to Israel about the birth of Jeshua.

"We went by first names only in those days, but we still had to be so cautious. Jeshua's first years were spent in Egypt where he was enrolled in various schools and, of course, in the mystery of the ancients there. He also studied the Torah, under Joseph's tutelage, and learned to read Hebrew. This was written in Greek, a form of cuneiform, and then the great language of Latin, and of course our native tongue, Aramaic.

"Jeshua read volumes and volumes of material, but he also would like to play and teach the other children. He was a natural-born teacher. He was very handsome to the point of almost looking a little bit effeminate, and that was because he embodied both the Divine Masculine and Divine Feminine traits.

"My child, Jeshua, was like no other in my mind and in the mind of my husband. Joseph kept these things in his heart and so did my mother, Anna. She did accompany us just a short while on the journey but was not able to continue all the way to Egypt. At that time there were pressing matters at the home for her, so she stayed on in Nazareth to keep things going."

"So it is. We bless you for listening today.

"We are Mother Mary and Mary Magdalene!"

Mother Mary, watercolor by Marcia McMahon c.

www.dianaspeakstotheworld.com

Chapter 30 Grandmother Anna Recalls the Birth of Jeshua in Bethlehem

Anna: "Many of you reading this were there at the birth, either in the spirit form or with us in the larger community of the Essenes at the time. It is true that the star shone brightly and this was a comet hovering directly overhead for about a month in December. Everyone sensed the situation that Jeshua was in. My grandson, Jeshua was the promised child and yet from his birth he began to experience this terrible threat. Of course we did everything possible to protect him.

"I walked some distance with Mary to guard her and be with her by her side until we all reached a place near the sea where Joseph of Arimathea came with a ship to collect them. They were so alone in the world, yet there was a Jewish community in Alexandria that was large and very cosmopolitan by ancient standards. In that day, among many different varieties of Jewish and Egyptian people, they settled into a small home where Joseph could continue his work in carpentry. Joseph was also an elder at that time in the temple. I missed them terribly—Mary, Joseph and Jeshua—but I had other children to attend to and these children now needed my attention in Nazareth.

"Today, if you go to the Church in Nazareth—the Church of Saint Mary—you can still see our large home. It contained generous arches, had many rooms and open spaces. At the time I remembered it as grand, in spite of the humbleness of Joachim. We had servants and gardens and assistance for comfortable things. Nazareth was our home, but we had to be very secretive about our lives.

"There was an inner network of messengers that would run from village to village with coded messages. Someone else would translate that code before we could read the message. That is how I received my updates from Mary and Joseph in Egypt along with the news of little Jeshua. He was growing swiftly into quite the fine young man and attending high schools there. How I wanted to go to visit him, as I had been to Egypt previously to the Temple of Isis! However, my duties as mother of the rest of the children were an all-consuming. I understood that my mission was to be the mother figure for the larger clan of the Essenes.

"This was all rather well-coordinated through our networks. We found out that Mary and Joseph arrived safely in Alexandria, where they were living a secretive and private life and where the Romans couldn't find them. It was safe for Jeshua to be able to attend school and to grow. As I understand it, Jeshua received training in many languages and began reading the Torah at a very young age. He could also write. He got along well with his classmates, but he was always teaching. And he would play games and tricks with people, so Mary told me.

"They were away for about ten years before I got word through our network, Mary would be returning. It was now safe to come home to Nazareth. So, when we heard news that their ship may have arrived at the port near another town—I think it was called Nabulus—we went forth in caravan with provisions to meet them. They certainly would have been tired from the ship's journey! All their life belongings came with them, which was no easy task in those days.

"By then, more of my children had grown up. We had three boys and three girls, Mary being my first. Some of her brothers and sisters accompanied us on our way. We were met with jubilation once more to reunite, while Jeshua had grown into a fine young man. Mary had other children by that time, so there were two sisters and three brothers, with James being the eldest. There was Josie, then Laura and Hannah, and one more male child. It was indeed wonderful to meet my entire family and see them as they were growing up. We embraced with great joy, and then helped the family to resettle in Nazareth. They lived close to our home."

(**Author's note:** There is a home in Nazareth being excavated thought to belong to the actual family of Mary, Joseph and Jeshua.)

"I can remember well a birthday party that was being held in which Jeshua was honored. Mary, her sisters and her brothers, Jeshua's uncles, myself and Joachim. Joseph and all the other relatives from the village were invited to attend. The gift given was a special box. This box was jeweled and it dated from the time of the wise men. It was precious and it contained some objects to remind him of just who he was. It was not private and had been created as a ceremony between my daughter, myself and Jeshua's father, Joseph. It contained various oils, while the box itself was made of gold with rubies around it. It was presented by one of the astrologers at his birth.

"Jeshua looked at it in a quizzical way and then he looked at his father, Joseph, and there was a great deal of expectation between them. Being our eldest he was almost ready to go down for the traditional ceremony.

"Many children from the village came to a picnic, particularly those who needed something to eat or drink. Many were around Jeshua's age, and they did not see the gift that was a held in a separate ceremony. The table was set with many fruits and vegetables, some fish and different types of breads. It was a warm, bright and sunny day although it was close to his time of birth in December. The weather had been unusually beautiful for his celebration. Jeshua was dressed in a long white robe which he received as a gift. Mary was silently in tears, but everyone was feasting on the food left over from the harvest. After their procurement of wine or an apple, the children ran free. Jeshua played with the children. We had invited all of them that were at the feast, about a hundred or so children from the village. One would think that this would have endeared Jeshua to the village boys, but because he was so well-educated and handsome, there was much envy and even some bullying of Jeshua. They were jealous because of the rumor that he was the Messiah. He used to be mocked, but he would simply smile and say nothing.

"When Jeshua was a little older there was a false accusation made by a woman in the village, who claimed that he had made advances toward her. We all knew this could not be true, for Jeshua was a good boy. A gang came at night to talk to him and dragged him out of the house. He was beaten very badly and nearly died. If it weren't for Mary and our nursing care, he would not have lived.

"Jeshua had to be kept confined to the house and nursed for he had broken bones and many wounds. At this time, he went into a deep identity crisis. Many young boys have an identity crisis, but this was especially so for my grandson, because he was destined to be a Messiah. Mary searched and read the Torah and the scriptures and, of course, he did a great deal of soul-searching. Jeshua didn't speak to me or Mary about it because he was still at the house recovering. I'm sure it was a dismal thought to have to play this role and be the victim.

"Joseph had tried to counsel Jeshua to be stronger and to build up his physical strength and, therefore, be able to defend himself, but Jeshua felt that his studies demanded more attention than his physical physique. He was a tall and thin young man. He liked people, but it took him quite a few years to recover after he had returned from his time in the temple.

"Next, Jeshua became curious about other religions and other people when he met travellers in the village who had come all the way from both the near East and the Far East. He had a strong desire to visit and study world religions there. He also had a strong desire about the Torah and everyday Torah reading was his main practice. He used to teach his brothers and sisters the beginnings of his teaching as recorded in the Bible, but his brothers and sisters were more interested in growing up and leaving normal lives. They all found him a bit odd. As I said before, raising a Messiah on my part as his grandmother while Anna, and Mary's part as his mother, was not an easy task. There were also other children to manage so both of our lives were very busy and complex. Much of it was focused on day-to-day survival.

"Sometime later Jeshua petitioned his father for permission to visit and study with the Eastern masters. He had heard the stories of resurrection and the stories of the great Yogi, Babaji. He felt that if he studied all, as the Messiah he would be able to address all the needs of everyone. It was out of love that he desired to go and seek inner knowledge and to find different traditions and religions.

"One must understand, of course, that Joseph was reluctant. Joseph wanted Jeshua to stay at home and help with the family business. He should also study the Torah night and day and become proficient in Hebrew and Aramaic, which Joseph already was. Joseph and Jeshua always seemed to have a conflict regarding his role.

"Later, in about his eighteenth or nineteenth year, Jeshua felt well enough to make arrangements to go by caravan to visit what is now Iran and Persia, and then move south to India on the Silk Road. He had to leave by night because father Joseph did not fully support or agree with the mission. Jeshua had saved enough money to clothe and feed himself for a month or two, and he had made arrangements for this trip for a long time.

"After he left, Mary was broken-hearted at her oldest son having gone so suddenly in the night, but he did leave word where he was going and when he was expected back. Joseph was distraught about his eldest son's decision and went off to find him. Many messengers were sent out for word on where he was and how far he had travelled in the first few days. However, it was not to be that Joseph would stop him.

"Joseph was furious. There was little he could do, as he was unable to find Jeshua. I believe Jeshua may have travelled under a different name while he was still in Israel, then crossed over into Jordan and went south to hear a prophet. He was a brave and very independent young man. He had discussed this with Mary, and I knew that he wanted to learn the ways of the East, to meet a real master, to learn to meditate, and accept people's teachings from all over the world. He was not alone in that he had been secretly married while away. This is something that we only learned about later.

"While he was away, Jeshua met a Samaritan woman, Miriam of Tyana, and they were married shortly before they left. The visit to India was their honeymoon. It had all been planned by spirit for some time, that Jeshua would make this trip. Meeting Miriam on the road as he did, and then having been married in private, made it all-the more mysterious and unique.

"Jeshua had been engaged to Mary of Bethany, and that seemed to have fallen apart when he left for India, and we later learned about the other woman and his marriage proposal. We were dismayed to learn that he had married into a Samaritan tribe to this woman who seemingly came out of nowhere. Mother Mary was present at the wedding and so was I, but it was otherwise kept from general knowledge throughout our village, and from the elders who wanted nothing further to do with Jeshua. So, the couple left in haste after a beautiful ceremony held secretly in Cana. That is why your Bible will tell you that there was a wedding in Cana where they had no wine left, and where Jeshua performed the miracle of the wine.

"Mary of Bethany was his friend from childhood, and so was Martha. They were daughters of Uncle Joseph of Arimathea. They frequented our family reunions, and Mary of Bethany was totally broken-hearted when Jeshua left with another woman, although I feel she was there at the wedding. She put on a happy face for Jeshua, but I could see the heartache in her eyes. She had dark brown, piercing eyes and she was small in stature. While Martha was also petite, she had blue eyes and was practical. Some of the people wept for joy at the wedding, but Mary and I wept because we didn't know what would become of this new couple and how they would fare outside of Israel, knowing his destiny was to the be the Messiah to Israel.

"As I said before, in the beginning of my discourse on our darling grandson Jeshua, being a Messiah was no easy task, nor was raising one nor was having one in the family. However, he was a true joy and he had grown into a fine man.

"Jeshua departed in the caravan with Miriam and ventured into the unknown. It was a frightful time for both Mother Mary and me. We prayed for him and, of course, we had our secret emissaries who would report back to us on rare occasions. We worried for his life and we worried that he might not be able to fulfill his mission because we felt the mission was to Israel. And so it was.

"His father, Joseph, shunned him in this entire adventure and marriage. I felt that they had to leave because they could not fit into our society any longer, and Jeshua had many reasons for wanting to study with the great masters of the Far East. We had many talks about it before he left. Everything had happened so quickly, but while we felt a desire to control his destiny, only he could do so. Now that he was a fully-grown man, we had to release him to his soul's destiny and his desire. As Jeshua was rather young when he married, we worried about how Miriam would fare on the road. We barely knew her, but we liked her very much, and she was related to a tribe of the Canaanites and to Judah.

"Mary was always loving and supportive of whatever Jeshua wanted, even though she tried to control her own innermost feelings about this dubious marriage. She so totally adored him that she went along with everything.

"Joseph was much more skeptical because Jeshua was not following the letter of the law, while fulfilling his destiny to Israel here at home. This was a contested issue only because the other children felt that Jeshua should also stay home and help Joseph with the carpentry work. But Jeshua was never meant to be a carpenter despite the fact that he could do it very well.

"Mother Mary and Joseph lived on in Nazareth with us while Joseph organized his carpentry business nearby, and it continued to excel. He had much wood carving to do, as well as house building and the making of chairs and other furniture. It was very hard labor, but things were done with each session under Joseph's oversight.

"We all prayed to the angels for Jeshua and Miriam's safety, and I'm sure he ran into many encounters on the road after leaving for the East.

"I was never completely informed of all the experiences that Jeshua had in India, but there are other books that will tell the story. It was many years before I saw my grandson again and he had grown in wisdom and in the size of his family."

Concluding remarks

Anna: "Jeshua was my amazing grandson, a true Prince of Peace. In all my lifetimes here on Earth I have attempted to imitate this great master who was misunderstood and crucified for no reason at all.

"I was supportive of his mission throughout my life as Grandmother Anna and continued my work with the Essenes and various communities throughout France and then in Glastonbury, England, where I settled. I had been the grandmother of the tribe and returned to a place nearest my heart in England. I can only say that the story is too long to be told in just one book and, therefore, I conclude with this thought:

"You are each an inner prince or princess. Although I served as Princess Diana, I also served as mother and grandmother to the most amazing person that has walked the Earth. He is still very precious to me. I shall never forget the time I had in Israel, France and England, and all the family that we served in the larger community, the followers, and also the adventures we had. Jeshua was a true blessing, and I ask you to get in touch with your own inner prince or princess, for this is where you find heaven and peace, as he taught."

Chapter 31 Joseph of Arimathea Reveals the Secrets of Jeshua's Tomb

Interview in heaven at Bob Murray's home May 2, 2018

Channeled by Marcia McMahon

Marcia: "I surround myself in the light as I call upon Father Bob and Joseph of Arimathea. Hi, Father Bob, is this a good time to connect with you?"

Father Bob Murray: "Yes, as a matter of fact it is. I just saw your lovely friend, Princess Diana, and she sends her warmest regards, of course. I will contact Joseph and invite him over, as well. You go into a state of deep relaxation as you travel out on your silver cord to discuss further information with Joseph of Arimathea. I will set up a barrier of white light protection in my home and you do the same for yourself. Take a few minutes now to relax."

Bob Murray: "Marcia, the Christ Consciousness prepares me for what I'm about to receive through Joseph of Arimathea, regarding any new information that sheds light on what truly happened to Jeshua in the Tomb, and how it may be useful for today's time."

Marcia: "I am, of course, a believer in the traditional story, but that can be temporarily suspended for the purposes of investigating truth. May God's guiding hand and light envelop me with Princess Diana, Mother Mary, Mary Magdalene, Archangel Michael and Jeshua himself."

Father Bob: "I am going to put my hands on a Bible so that we are safely surrounded. And, I'm calling in the light of the Christ consciousness and my old friend, Joseph of Arimathea.

"This information you're about to hear will be a little bit unusual. Just keep an open mind and make no judgments until the session is over. Remember to always surround yourself in the light as you remain connected to your silver cord. You may experience sights and sounds, you may enter the tomb, you may see what others saw and felt at the tomb, and you may be led into an experience of how it all evolved."

Joseph of Arimathea: "I am here. I'm always available at Bob's request, your request, or any sincere request as the search for truth and knowledge is always greatly appreciated. I know what you're about to ask me, and I will settle in to the other chair adjacent to Bob. I tell Marcia to go back to the time when you and Mary were in the tomb, and you were anointing the body of our dearly beloved Jeshua. You experienced nothing out of the ordinary, you are a healer, and so is Mary."

Marcia: "Yes, I'm back there. I'm seeing Jeshua's poor body. There's blood everywhere and I am so horrified at this incident. I don't know how this could possibly happen to our Messiah. I'm wiping his wounds clean. Mary is applying myrrh and aloe along with Mother Mary. I see that you are here, too, and so is Nicodemus. The tomb is not closed. There is a shaft of light coming through the doorway."

Joseph: "Yes, there is enough light to see by, though we all had simple candles because it was growing dark. Both Nicodemus and I hoisted his body down and gave it to Mother Mary and she wept for the rest of the afternoon. She was in such shock she could barely perform the cleansing of the body. We were all in shock at this horrific site. When the sun had set, the stone still had not been rolled away. We had access to the tomb until later that evening, when the Romans came to shut it off. There were two specific healers brought into the tomb, who have been holding light with crystals, and who also brought aromatic herbs and spices for the body of Jeshua. At this time, you will also notice that Jeshua had entered the spirit realm.

"His body has been laid to rest. Mother Mary, I and the other two healers all worked on the body of Jeshua. We called for the three Archangels: Michael, Gabriel and, of course, Raphael, the Healer, who is known as Razihel in our time. We laid our hands on the head and feet while the healers worked, administering both energetic healing and solar healing. There were crystals resting at his head and feet and also near, but not on, the wounds."

Marcia: "Joseph, can you identify the names of the two healers? I'm feeling that one was Miriam and possibly the other a friend of Jeshua,"

Joseph: "You are quite correct. Miriam was part of the secret committee. Mother Mary was there holding the light. The anointing and cleansing had taken place, but there was a quickening. There had been a faint pulse and the faint pulse had begun to beat once more after about five hours."

Marcia: "Was it Laura who was involved in the healing?"

Joseph: "Yes, Laura Claire was involved, as would have been Jeshua's other sister. My home just behind the tomb had a secret entrance at that time, although it was a rock-hewn tomb. Another secret entrance was located out the back, which has been covered over and sealed permanently. You won't see it in the garden tomb today as it was a top-secret operation.

"During the day Saturday we all sent healing energy to Jeshua for his revival. There were three strategic crystals placed in Jerusalem and right behind my house. At about midnight there was a flash of light that was emitted from the tomb much like lightning! It left the indelible impression of Jeshua's light body on the cloth, which today is known as the Shroud of Turin. This is a genuine artifact among others we've discussed before."

Marcia: "Thank you, Joseph. Were the angels invoked or called upon to send healing and light energy to Jeshua?"

Joseph: "The angels were constantly at work and they contributed to the light. Archangel Metatron, the master of sacred geometry, also attended, to rearrange Jeshua's subatomic particles so that he could be both in his physical and his light-body. Lord Maitreya had been over-lighting Jeshua throughout his entire three-year Ministry! Maitreya has a direct lineage to the Buddha. Jeshua received his fifth initiation on the cross. He had experienced great suffering, but in our opinion, he did not die, but rather went into the underworld to rescue the souls that were there waiting for the light to lead the way up out of the hell planes.

"And on that great night, Jeshua had his subatomic particles and atoms rearranged with that flash of light that emitted from the tomb. If you would light up a skyscraper today at midnight this is what happened at the tomb. Most of the healers had rested, but I was a witness to it.

"When you and Mary returned to the tomb on Sunday morning, the first day of the week, Mary was stable enough and so were you, to assist Jeshua with your intent to complete the healing of his wounds. Mary had brought aloe and myrrh. Calendula was used to seal the wounds and so was myrrh to sterilize them as well. When the flash of lightning occurred, it seems to have dissolved his earthly particles and made the ascension particles more prevalent. Since his atoms were spinning now at a higher vibration, that is how Jeshua was able to appear and disappear, and why he looked so different to Mary.

"This also explains why his body was never found. There are a series of stories about people who went to bury the body elsewhere, to protect Jeshua and let him move on. But we did our part to rearrange Jeshua's energy portal as much as we could. We had to turn it over to the angels to do the rest of the healing, as it was quite instantaneous and fast. So, in a way of speaking, Jeshua technically only died for about five hours. He then resurrected himself through the help of healers and the archangels, who are the Elohim, the Gods of this particular Milky Way Galaxy.

"Your new friend will be able to testify to this transformation that Jeshua underwent. He had practiced for this in the temples of Egypt and in previous lifetimes, but also in his stay in Egypt, where he was under the care of his father.

"By that time, I had replaced Jeshua's father and I was his father figure. Jeshua felt very persecuted for his fine work, and there was a misunderstanding between us, but I did the best I could to assist in the rescue of Jeshua and to revive him from the cross. It was quite an ordeal for him."

Marcia: "Oh, I feel like I'm touching the Divine as I sit here with you, Joseph of Arimathea. You are beginning to glow with the light that is exactly like Jeshua's, and as I used to glow after he reappeared to us in his resurrection form."

Joseph: "You are correct, my sister Martha. I do have a glow about me through the pride of my eye, Jeshua. I have soul aspects on the Earth plane right now that will remember the facts of this. I would advise you to reach them with this message as soon as possible. However, I want to say that this information will be very uncomfortable to some people and, therefore, do not worry about it.

"It was beyond your ability as Martha to understand how such a resurrection could be accomplished, and we were not sure if it would happen. Most of this divine solar healing light you would describe as radiation today. Radiation was emitted from the sun and then carried by the angels Metatron and Michael to the very cellular structure of our beloved Jeshua. This was so that he could continue teaching the disciples and his friends and family from afar.

"Jeshua had to leave Palestine, for he was a wanted man, and so various rumors were spread around to confuse the people. The Romans were particularly eager to remove Jeshua, as well as the Sanhedrin at home, of whom I was a part. I did not vote against my beloved adopted son, but I did all in my best to save him.

"It was known that this would happen for some time, as the crystals in Jerusalem had been placed there from the time of Atlantis. What we refer to as a particle of the Ark of the Covenant was in my house, as well. It was powerful, and in a tightly locked place. It had to be activated and then brought into the tomb."

Marcia: "Thank you, Joseph of Arimathea. I wonder if you could tell me more about remnants of the Ark of the Covenant that were sealed in right behind the tomb? It was said, since ancient times, that the Ark of the Covenant emitted a radiation of sorts that was quite dangerous. This was in the form of activated crystals."

Joseph: "Yes, my child, that is correct. Only I and a few others knew about the presence of the remnants of the ark. The ark is also still in existence today in a place in Ethiopia where there is a sacred Church and shrine built to it. There is a high level of radiation emitting from there, which is dangerous to the average human. This is the solar encapsulation of radiation that was emitted, which assisted Jeshua to resurrect his body.

"This is all secret knowledge up until now and is available only to a very few. The whole operation was top-secret, as we wanted Jeshua to continue in his travels to England, and in his teaching all the way to Scotland. And then, of course, you heard about his travels to India."

Marcia: "Well Joseph, I've had a lot to think about and I've enjoyed my cup of tea and your story about the tomb. I've entered into the tomb. I scarcely noticed as the time flew by again, with the wonderful hospitality of Father Bob Murray. May I shake your hand and absorb some of your radiant glow, Joseph?"

Joseph: "I would be honored, my lady, to not only shake your hand but give you a fatherly embrace, and I will impart my glow to send healing rays for your total healing."

Marcia: "And I'm asking Father Bob now if I may also have a handshake or a warm hug?

Father Bob moves forward closer to me, then he holds my hands, and places his hands on my shoulders for a healing.

"You are welcome, Marcia, anytime that you want to visit in my office to do some time travel. I have other work awaiting me, and I'm writing quite a bit through my son James. You can find my work online, so please use the citation at the end of the chapter. It was great seeing you, Marcia, you're looking as healthy as ever, and I know Joseph's glowing healing will be with you for quite some time."

Marcia: "Well, I hate to leave, but I must get dinner and finish the day back on Earth. Thank you both for your time and this little visit! It was unforgettable and extraordinary."

Reference:

Murray, Robert. www.thestarsstillshine.com

Father Bob Murray, affectionately called father, is not a priest. He is a spiritual leader in many ways. Father Bob's works have appeared in all of my books on Princess Diana and John Lennon. He was a mentor to me somewhat while he was on the Earth plane, even though we had not met. His fine work can be found at www.thestarsstillshine.com his fine website. Bob's son, James Murray, writes, does art work, and continues his work in channeling and the E publication of the e-zine *The Stars Still Shine*.

Chapter 32 Mary Magdalene's Final Request, Mary Magdalene and Mother Mary Speak, A Plea for Women around the World

Marcia: "I am calling upon the light to surround me at all times. I ask for my mind to be cleared of any worries or debris. I ask for the Divine Feminine in the form of Mary Magdalene, Mother Mary and all the angels of the Divine Feminine. They're here!

"Mary Magdalene, I would like to ask you, since this is your book, what you wish as the title? I also request your final thoughts on your major life contributions as Jeshua's wife, and his primary teacher of the Inner Way Mastery School."

Mary Magdalene: "My sweet sister of the light. It is with great respect that you have compiled this book of sayings of mine, memories, past life regressions and details that are yet unknown to the public. I say to you that there is more yet to be uncovered in the following days of regressions with your two friends that you have recently met. Do you choose to include these in the book, as it is still not quite finished?

"I would like you to ask your friends to support a Divine Feminine Reiki group and healing group, which we could call the Goddess Circle. I would like to ask you to reach out, once you have the book published, to various groups in your community and surrounding area, and send the message of mine. I think the title of the book should be, Mary Magdalene Speaks, the Holy Grail, the Bloodline and Secrets of the Divine Feminine!"

Marcia: "Mary, is there anything you want to say as your parting words in the book?"

Mary: "Both Mother Mary and I are grateful for your penmanship and your dedication to the Divine Feminine. We ask that your participants commit themselves to the practice of unconditional motherly love, and to a sisterly love for each other and for all. You will be grounding new groups by the end of summer, and I asked for retreats concerning contributions that I made as Saint Mary Magdalene. Mother Mary also wishes to speak more with you and through you and into your groups, in helping to ground the Divine Feminine and making the great plan of divine light of the feminine available to more people who are open to the rose of my love!

"I will always remain in love with Jeshua in the higher realms, even as I have taken on many soul aspects as Mary in this current Earth realm. Yes, we are here with you and the suffering of women all over the world. I really want to uplift women in a spiritual way, which was my original assignment from Jeshua. Many know that I was denigrated to that of repentant harlot, and my work in my gospels was never included in the biblical canon. I would like to see that reversed to include my words, my gospel again in the biblical canon. Other women ministers may take this on in time, as I am influencing them. I am also influencing the entire world to wake up to the justice and the peace of the woman.

"I am tired of seeing women torn apart by the patriarchal male societies into which they're born, particularly in the Middle East and in other repressive cultures. In Jeshua's vision for women, he felt that women, men and children are all equals, and everyone was an equal. He believed in nonviolence, he believed in sharing the world's wealth, shared in common, but simply sharing with friends and living in communities.

"For centuries the Catholic Church has hoarded her wealth, and yet lived in community with one another. Many of the monks and nuns dedicated to my memory have lived very well by living my truth. But they have not expressed themselves in the full sunshine of romantic love and, so, something has always gone missing in the convents and the abbeys, especially here in the United States.

"Jeshua never asked anyone to be celibate, and the celibacy is a hard vow. There are so many errors in the current Christian tradition that it would be impossible to erase the damage that was done to women and men. They made God separate and outside of you, but the God and Goddess are within you. Jeshua taught so many eons ago that the kingdom of God is within you. History is told by the winners, and now we are reshaping history to become her story.

"I commend you as we stand with and for women across the world, to help them out of patriarchal systems of thought and repression. I stand for the light, I stand for the goodness in a woman, and I stand for motherhood and sexual expression. It is my wish that all women everywhere finally hear my voice, as I wish and long for the day that all my gospels are rediscovered and published in the world.

"It is my wish that the Churches accept my teachings into their teaching, and that women could be taught how to use intuition, as you do. Men as well could also be initiated into the Divine Feminine. They should learn to appreciate the mother, the Divine Sophia. So it is.

"I close, not permanently but just for a time, to allow you peace and to allow your healing. All of you out there who hear my voice know that I stand with you in any crisis. We are Mary Magdalene and Mother Mary, the two mothers of the world. We love you as our children. We cherish you, and we will teach you. Just learn to ask within and we will come to you and you will know us in your hearts.

"I am Mary Magdalene. I wish that you hear the voices of the angels whenever you feel hurt or any way in need."

"And, I am Mother Mary. We bless you all."

Bibliography

Angelo, J. *"The Healing Wisdom of Mary Magdalene,"* 2015. Bear and Co. www.bearandcompany.com

BBS radio.com https://bbsradio.com/peacefulplanet. www.Bbsradio.com, founders Doug and Don Newsome host a wide variety of holistic, psychic, New Age, Spiritual, ecology and political shows since 2005. Marcia McMahon still hosts the Peaceful Planet show every other Sat at 6 pm CST, Marcia still interviews authors for her acclaimed works, the *Jesus Holy Grail Mysteries.*

Babaji https://yoganandasite.wordpress.com/2018/07/06/mahavatar-babaji-supreme-guru-of-srf-yss-yogis-paramahansa-yogananda/

Chapin, L. Divine Union, *The Love Story of Jesus and Mary Magdalene.* 2017.

Crop Circle Connector, www.cropcircleconnector.com, image retrieved June, 2017

Cannon, D. *Jesus and the Essenes.* Published by Ozark Mountain Publishing www.ozarkmountainpublishing.com, 1999

The Gospel of Mary. http://gnosis.org/library/marygosp.htm

The Gospel of Mary Magdalene is part of the gnostic gospels.

Heartsong, C. & Clemett, C.A. *Anna Voices of the Magdalenes, A Sequel to Anna, Grandmother of Jesus*, 2004. Hay House, Carlsbad, www.hayhouse.com

Heartsong, C. *Anna, Grandmother of Jesus*, 2017.

Holy Bible. New Revised Standard Version

Jacobovici, S., & Wilson, B. *The Lost Tomb of Jesus*, 2007. *The Lost Gospel: Decoding the Ancient Text that Reveals Jesus' Secret Marriage to Mary the Magdalene*, 2014.

King, K. *The Gospel of Mary of Magdala, Jesus and the First Woman Apostle.* Polebridge Press, Santa Rosa, CA, 2003.

Kirkel, M. *Mary Magdalene Beckons; Join the River of Love. Into the Heart Creations*, Santa Fe, NM, 2012. www.intotheheart.org

Kenyon, T. *The Magdalen Manuscript*, 2006

Le Loup, J-Y. *The Gospel of Mary Magdalene.* Inner Traditions, 2002. www.innertraditions.com

The Lord's Prayer in Aramaic

http://www.wayofmastery.com/pathway/the_aramaic_jesus/3248.html

https://www.youtube.com/watch?v=MAEIrp4MFBE

Martin E. *King of Travelers, Jesus Lost Years in India*, by Yellow Hat Publishing, Reno Nevada 2008. NBC Universal's Studios, Sundance Channel www, picked up the distribution of Jesus in India. Jesus-In-India_ the-movie.com.

Meier, B. *Talmud of Jmmanuel*, 2005. It was possibly found by Billy Meier and another Palestinian archaeologist, in the Palestinian occupied territory. Meier translated this gospel into several languages.

McCannon, T. *Return of the Divine Sophia: Healing the Earth through the Lost Wisdom Teachings of Jesus, Isis and Mary Magdalene.* Bear and Co. 2015 Rochester , VT, www.bearandcompanybooks.com

McMahon, M. *The Grail Mysteries* Peaceful Planet CD mp3 recordings of Ed Martin, Joanna Prentis and Stuart Wilson, Robert Murray and other authors. Available through email

Marciadi2002@yahooo.com   or
www.dianaspeakstotheworld.com

McMahon, Marcia.   www.dianaspeakstotheworld.com 2001. *Princess Diana's Message of Peace by Marcia McMahon, 2003, and With Love from Diana, Queen of Hearts,* Eternal Rose Publishing, 2005. Available from the author's website and on amazon.com. *Ascension Teachings with Archangel Michael,* 2013 e-book, and new paperback version, 2017. *Notes from John Messages from Across the Universe,* 2013, Eternal Rose Publishing.

www.enlightenedhypnosis.net. Marcia offers self esteem, cancer side by side hypnosis, as well as past lives regression via Skype and at her office in Illinois.

www.divineconnectionswithreiki.com Marcia McMahon offers Angelic Reiki training called Angelic Awakening as well as Reiki Attunements, Usui lineage, and Biomat Reiki sessions. She hosts a monthly Reiki goddess circle and Magdalene retreats. Readings with Archangel Michael are available by reaching the author.

Murray, R. *The Stars Still Shine, A Surprising Journey through the Afterlife. Vol 1 and 2* Published www.thestarsstillshine.com. Father Bob Murray's fine work can be found at www.thestarsstillshine.com. Bob's son, James Murray, writes, does artwork, and continues his work in channeling and the E publication of the e-zine *The Stars Still Shine!*

Prentis, J, & Wilson, S. *Power of the Magdalene*, 2008, *The Essenes, Children of the Light*, 2007, the *Magdalene Version*, 2012 published by Ozark Mountain Publishing. www.ozarkmountainpublishing.com

Starbird, M. *Mary Magdalene, Bride in Exile*, 2005 www.inner-traditions.com. Margaret has appeared on the peaceful planet show and has proven through Biblical research the Magdalene was indeed married to Jeshua ben Joseph.

Stevenson, Ian. *Twenty Cases Suggestive of Reincarnation* . Reincarnation Research https://www.near-death.com/reincarnation/research/ian-stevenson.html

Yogananda, P. *The Yoga of Jesus*. Self Realization Fellowship, 2004. Yogananda explores Jesus' travels in India as a youth.

The Garden Tomb, Jerusalem

https://en.wikipedia.org/wiki/The_Garden_Tomb - Selah_Merril,_Samuel_Gobat,_Conrad_Schick 1.2.6 Ernest Renan

Wikipedia, *The Garden Tomb found in 1887*, https://en.wikipedia.org/wiki/The_Garden_Tomb, retrieved April 11, 2018. Many Protestants believe this to be the actual tomb of Jeshua, but carbon 14 dating goes back to the 4-5th century.

Marcia McMahon

About the Author

Marcia McMahon, M.A.

BA, Ursuline College

MA, Case Western Reserve University and The Cleveland Institute of Art

Diana Gallery Online:

www.dianaspeakstotheworld.com
www.divineconnectionswithreiki.com
www.enlightenedhypnosis.net,
www.MasterywithArchangelmichaelandmarymagdalene.com

Marcia is an accomplished artist, retired professor of Art History, and Spiritual Teacher. She has published four other books two on Princess Diana, one on John Lennon and one with Archangel Michael.

Marcia teaches **Angelic Awakening** classes to accompany her Reiki practice. She is an internationally recognized angel intuitive/psychic channel and author. Her books are channeled inspiration from Princess Diana and John Lennon on how to create a world of peace and unity. Marcia was named in Who's Who in America for 2018. She is known for her former show, the highly acclaimed **Peaceful Planet** on www.bbsradio.com. She is a nationally certified Hypnotist with NGH, and does past lives regression and Angelic Reiki. Marcia has overcome stage four breast cancer and remains well today. Marcia has been channeling Mother Mary, Mary Magdalene and Jesus since 2004. This is a compilation of those messages with past life regressions of her clients as well as her own past life. She continues to host Magdalene workshops everywhere in person and online, promoting a space to hold the sacred Chalice of the Divine Feminine.

Marcia channels Archangel Michael and has released *Ascension Teachings with Archangel Michael* (2012), a book explaining in clear words the Ascension process and Earth changes. Marcia's interviews have been heard on hundreds of programs on radio and TV. She has recently appeared on Hugh Riley's TV show *That Channel in Canada*!

Reach Marcia at marciadi2002@yahoo.com.

Made in the USA
Columbia, SC
03 February 2021